Freelance Writer's Handbook
Second Edition

by James Wilson

Loompanics Unlimited
Port Townsend, Washington

Neither the author nor the publisher assumes any responsibility for the use or misuse of information contained in this book. It is sold for entertainment purposes only. Be Warned!

Freelance Writer's Handbook,
Second Edition
© 2001 by James Wilson

Published by:
Loompanics Unlimited
PO Box 1197
Port Townsend, WA 98368
Loompanics Unlimited is a division of Loompanics Enterprises, Inc.
Phone: 360-385-2230
E-mail: service@loompanics.com
Web site: www.loompanics.com

ISBN 1-55950-212-6
Library of Congress Card Catalog Number 00-110746

Contents

Part II: Tools

Part III: Managing Your Career

Introduction

This book is a realistic look at writing for a living. It describes what the rewards are, as well as problems you may encounter. The purpose is to help you decide whether or not to give it a try, and if you decide to try it, to give you a running start. With this in mind, ask yourself:

Do you want to write?

Why?

Is it because you think it's an exciting career? Do you think it's glamorous, intellectual, emotionally rewarding, or perhaps, it pays well? It can be one or all of these, but there are some factors that you will need to take into consideration. Let's take a hard look at what writing has to offer to the person who wants to make it a career.

The writing field has been glamorized, as has photography and working for the airlines. You almost surely won't get rich. The field is terribly overcrowded, and the competition is stiff. You will also need luck — lots of luck.

You will find that there are a lot of myths about the writing field. This book will dispel them.

Within these pages you'll find a discussion of what tools you need to be a writer — the obvious, as well as the not so obvious.

This book will provide a basic understanding of the practical tactics that you will need to be a writer. There's a lot of nuts-and-bolts information that isn't usually available in one volume. In this book, you'll get the down-and-dirty facts about writing for pay. This book will help you discover the hidden pitfalls of the writer's market, and also potential errors you may encounter and ways that these may be avoided.

Let's also state what this book is not.

It's not a book on basic grammar. Let's hope that you were able to pick this up in school. It's also not a handbook on style. You can find a good basic guide to style in the excellent volume by Strunk.[1] This book is also not a listing of all of the publications and potential markets in the country. These change almost daily, therefore any such listing soon becomes obsolete.

This book is also not an effort to "sell" you on any equipment, service, school, or anything else that is available. This book contains no advertising, and doesn't owe anything to manufacturers or distributors of anything related to writers' needs. This means that you'll find in these pages an honest appraisal of some goods and services that relate to writing, including some warnings about what to avoid.

Now let's get into the vital details. Why did I write this book, and what makes me think I know enough to advise others about writing?

First, let's be up front about one thing. I wrote this book for the money. I'm not ashamed to admit it. This is how I earn my living. I enjoy my work. I feel that it's a worthwhile occupation that I can recommend to others.

What about my qualifications? My major in college was psychology, not journalism. I don't have a single creative writing course under my belt, and I've also never taken a correspondence course in writing. If you judge me by paper credentials, I don't have enough background to write a comment on a toilet wall. However, I have been earning my living by writing books and articles for over twenty years. I've had about seventy books published. I've also had almost a thousand magazine articles appear in print. These give me the background to lay out the facts for those who are considering writing for a living.

During the past twenty years, I've also made a number of mistakes, which means that I can advise beginning writers from first hand knowledge.

The success of the first edition and the passage of time have led to this second edition. Much has changed in the writing field, not always for the better, and it's worth the trouble to examine these changes to see how they affect the beginning writer as well as the experienced one. Summing up, technological developments including computers, digital photography, e-mail, electronic submission and e-publishing, have made it easier to perform some of the everyday tasks a writer undertakes, but this has led more people into the field, increasing the competition you'll have to face. These technological advances have eliminated or mitigated many problems that used to pose gut-wrenching dilemmas for writers. Overall, the picture for the beginner is a bit brighter today.

Let's begin by examining what writing for a living might hold for you, so that you can compare it with your present field. There are benefits and disadvantages, and only you can decide if they stack up in the right way for you.

Notes:

1. *The Elements of Style,* William B. Strunk, Jr., and E.B. White, New York, MacMillan, 1959.

Part I:
Starting Out

You've decided to try writing as a career. Where and how do you begin? What will you need? How do you break into the field? This section will deal with the basics, including what writing can do for you, how writers get paid, and surveying the potential market.

One point we'd better cover right away is how you begin. Do you buy your equipment, begin writing, and tell your current employer to take his job and shove it? No, that's not smart. A much safer way is to dip your toe into the water to find out if writing will work for you. Write a few articles in your spare time while still working your regular job, to keep a floor under your income.

While doing so, keep quiet about your writing. Don't brag about it at work, for at least two reasons. You don't want to give your employer the idea that you'll be leaving him soon. That could kick back at you if he decides to lay off people to cut costs. Also, don't give your fellow employees any reason to be jealous of you. Most of your fellow employees will be happy that you're striving for something better, but a few might not, and this could cause interpersonal problems for you.

As your career takes off, you can decide when to write full-time. That point is when your writing income approaches your salary. If possible, you might decide to cut back the hours you spend at your salaried job. Finally, you can make the break complete and spend all of your working hours writing.

Let's begin with these premises. Later, we'll get into the equipment you'll need and the fine points of managing your career.

Chapter One
The Benefits of Writing as a Career

What can writing do for you? The answer to this question depends on what you can do for yourself. There are some real advantages to earning a living by writing, and these are much more important than the glamorous image that some consider important.

Writing as a trade[1] has its advantages, but it's important to specify advantages in relation to something else. Let's say that writing has advantages compared to the "average job." What is the "average job?" With all of the occupations we find in our country, how can we even find anything to call "average?" Let's try, anyway.

The "average job" requires the employee to report to a certain place five days a week, to remain about eight hours each day, with breaks for lunch and perhaps coffee. The "average employee" works under supervision, taking orders from a lead man, foreman, manager, or other low-level supervisor. Whether he's happy on the job or not depends very much on the personality of this first-line supervisor. If he's a decent fellow, and treats his subordinates fairly, the employee has a good chance of being contented on the job. If he's a tyrant, and takes out his personality problems on his employees, they will suffer.

The person who reports to the "average job" has to commute to work. This may be easy, or an ordeal, depending on where he lives, how far from work it is, and commuting conditions. In some locales, commuting can be a horror. The "average" worker does not get paid for commuting.

The "average" worker also has to be in the company of certain people while working, people whom he usually does not choose, and with whom he must get along despite possible personality clashes. If the job is office or factory work, the circle of contacts is limited. If it's a "service occupation," which involves contact with the public, it can be a trial at times. Any store clerk or waiter knows what it's like to be confronted by an unreasonable member of the public.

The "average worker" also collects a paycheck each week or pay period. The withdrawals are already deducted, and the remainder is his to spend as he wishes.

The regular paycheck offers the illusion of security to the "average worker." Sometimes he finds out that it isn't as secure as he'd thought, especially when he gets laid off or "downsized." Length of service doesn't count for much. Neither does ability. When an employer declares bankruptcy the "average worker" is out on the street.

Similarly, the "average worker" can lose his job in other ways, not necessarily his fault. A "reorganization" or "downsizing" can deprive him of his livelihood. So can a slump in business, forcing a layoff. A merger is always a time of dread, because the new management can decide that certain employees are unnecessary. Company politics often determine who gets laid off, and the employee without a "connection" upstairs is the one who loses out.

The "average worker" may dream of promotion, with increased pay and more authority. It may seem to him that his situation will improve by moving up to a supervisory position where he'll be able to institute changes he feels are long overdue. If he wins a promotion, he'll find that he's caught in another squeeze, between management over him and employees under him. He'll be obligated to enforce rules he didn't originate, and with which he may even disagree. He'll find himself caught in the bind of responsibility without authority. This is why the "executive ulcer" is largely a myth. Executives don't get ulcers: they give them to their subordinates.

Finally, the average jobholder is on the short end, whatever he does. If he doesn't like his job, he's perfectly free to quit, as some employers love to remind their employees. If he does, the employer expects two weeks' notice. At layoff time, however, the employee may get only two minutes' notice.

What we've just drawn is a rough sketch, but it describes most of the jobs in this country. That's why so many people with this sort of employment are "wage slaves." Let's also remember that most editors work under these conditions. Now let's look at what it's like to be a writer.

Let's start by saying that we're considering only freelance writers. There are many writers who are journalists, newspaper and magazine reporters. They work for paychecks, and their working conditions vary greatly. The fortunate few are free to roam the world, sending home stories from the capitals of foreign countries and other places where there's news or a feature story. Most newspaper and magazine reporters are confined to home base, with a specified "beat" and a desk in the "bull pen," a sort of communal office with no privacy and too much noise. This is not to say that they can't find satisfaction in their work. Many do. Their situation, however is quite different from that of the freelance writer.

The freelance writer is by definition self-employed. This means that you will not collect a regular paycheck. At first sight this seems terribly insecure. That's because we've been programmed to think that security lies in a regular paycheck.

What self-employment really means is that you will have several diverse sources of income. No single source can cripple you economically unless you're imprudent enough to work for only one outlet. Having diverse incomes promotes a feeling of security. It provides independence. It can be very satisfying.

You also get your checks uncut. There are no withholdings, courtesy of the Internal Revenue Service. Instead, you pay "estimated taxes" quarterly. This requires an ability to manage money. This also allows depositing the money in a savings account and collecting interest on it while waiting for the due dates of estimated taxes, which is better than letting the government keep the interest, as the "wage slave" is forced to do.

You are also free to accept or decline assignments. While it's a mistake to be so arrogant as to decline assignments regularly, some publishers are so troublesome, for one reason or another, that it simply doesn't pay to write for them. With other sources of income, you can say "no thank you" to the problems.

Some tasks, such as interviewing a difficult personality, may be troublesome. Unlike the jobholder who has to bear up to difficult people daily, you can take this in stride. You know that once the interview is over and you have your material, you can depart and leave the problem behind you.

Unlike the majority of factory or office labor, there's variety built into the writer's work. Every manuscript is different, and requires different preparation. There may be a need to interview people, which can be both challenging and interesting. For the person with an inquiring mind, there's the joy of discovery, as often the writer learns something new with each manuscript.

Commuting is not a problem. Most freelancers work at home, and you probably will too. This frees you from the expense and the wear and tear of daily commuting. It's sometimes necessary to travel to an assignment, but this is usually during the off-hours. Overall, it's nice to "commute" by walking down the hall to the office.

You'll also find that many day-to-day expenses are tax-deductible. If you have to go to an interview, the post office, or buy stationery, it comes off your taxes, unlike commuting costs for the wage earner. You can deduct the cost of your home office, unlike the wage slave.

Your hours are usually your own. You don't have to follow a fixed schedule, you begin work when you please, and quit when you feel it's appropriate. That's the advantage of a flexible schedule. If one night you can't sleep, you can get up, walk down the hall, and go to work. If you feel tired one afternoon, you can simply rest, or go to the park or shopping center. Although you must have some self-discipline and try to follow normal business hours, you're much less constrained and usually won't feel like a prisoner on the job.

You also won't have to put up with moment-to-moment supervision, as in many workplaces. This doesn't mean that you're utterly free to do what you wish, as your occupation is taxing in many ways. It does mean freedom from much of what we call "office politics," which often complicate an otherwise pleasant work situation. It also means freedom from many of the face-to-face relationships that employees have to endure.

A priceless benefit is not having employees and the problems that go with hiring today. You'll be on your own, and work alone. There are no problems with workplace politics, accusations of discrimination, or being sued for harassment. No minority member, feminist, or homosexual can hassle the writer for not hiring him or her, or for unfair dismissal. This alone makes writing very attractive compared to other small business enterprises.

The writer's environment and work situation has its own characteristics and demands. It's vastly different from that of the "nine-to-fiver." For the minority of people who are self-starters and independent, it's very rewarding, and the rewards far outweigh the frustrations.

Notes:

1. Writing is a trade, not a profession. A profession requires a higher education as a prerequisite. While a higher education can help, it's not necessary, and most successful writers did not major in journalism or allied topics.

Chapter Two
Myths About Writing

There are many myths about writing, fostered mainly by those who stand to profit by taking dollars from would-be writers. Usually, they present a rosy picture of what a writer's life is like, and minimize the difficulties involved in entering and remaining in the field. These profiteers portray an image of "anyone can do it," as long as they subscribe to the writer's magazine, buy the textbooks, and send for the correspondence courses.

The Myth of Quick Success

Advertisements for various writing "schools" present a rosy picture of the prospects for success. It's very simple, according to them. Just send your money, complete the "ten easy lessons," and wait for the money to roll in.

This may be so for a very few. In some instances, it's a matter of luck. Luck plays more of a part in writing success than many writers want to admit. It doesn't bestow glory on a writer to say that he happened to be in the right place at the right time, but that's the way it works most of the time. This is typical in an overcrowded field, where there are many talented people seeking recognition and reward.

This doesn't mean that you should lie back and wait for the lucky break. Total passivity will also get you nothing.

You can, to a certain extent, "make your own luck." This means being aware of when good fortune knocks, and being prepared to exploit the event immediately. There's a saying, "Opportunity knocks only once." This, like most popular sayings, is questionable. The number of times opportunity knocks depends upon the person who's counting. What some see as an opportunity, others consider worthless. Some people fail to recognize and exploit opportunities that fall into their laps. Others jump at everything that looks like an opportunity, failing to discriminate between real and spurious ones.

If you're considering a writing career, you also have to consider the chances of failure. The world is full of talented writers who simply have never "made it," for various reasons. Some are factors under individual control, and others nobody can control. We'll look at these and tie them together in later chapters.

The Myth of the Fair Minded Editor

Some writer's magazines promote this myth, presenting the picture of the editor as a benevolent master who'll make his decisions wisely and give you an even break. This is the view that the "writer's" magazines and the writer's how-to books present. They have to convey an optimistic view to sell their publications. As we'll see, the real picture is never that simple.

One writer's magazine came out with a cover story, "Do Editors Steal Ideas?" This topic is of serious concern to any writer who has ever sent in a query and had it rejected, only to find the publication running a startlingly similar article shortly thereafter. The author of this article denied stoutly that editors steal ideas, but that isn't surprising. It would be discouraging to the readers to admit that they might ever be cheated or otherwise mistreated by an editor, and that might turn some of them off writing completely. They might be so turned off that they might not even renew their subscriptions to the magazine.

The reality is quite different. Editors sometimes do steal ideas. Sometimes they steal an entire article.[1] This shouldn't be surprising. There are unethical people in the media, just as there are in other fields.

Editors are human, and they have their share of dead-heads, as in other occupations. They're also subject to pressures that impair their effectiveness, and their ability to make accurate judgments of the work they receive. In this book, we'll examine very closely the pressures that affect an editor. We'll also assess their effect on your chances of success.

The Myth That Success Depends Entirely on a Set Procedure

The fundamental fact is that you have to know how to write first. This is the hard part, and there's no getting away from it. There's no easy way to ensure success, especially if you don't know how to put words together, and there are no "five step programs" or "ten easy lessons" to help you learn. Many Americans simply don't understand basic grammar and syntax. They were short-changed in schools that devote more attention to "social studies" and volleyball than to sound basic education. You might find this hard to believe, but take a look at immigrants who got their education abroad. You'll probably find some who speak better English than some native-born Americans.

Closer to home, check out your friends. If you've moved to another city during your lifetime, count how many of your old friends write to you. They may phone, but you'll get very few letters. Many Americans have writing skills so poor that they can't compose a friendly letter.

The Myth That a Writer's Course Assures Success

The falsity of this myth is immediately evident from scanning the ads. These schools feature "name" writers on their "board of directors," because the "name" writers get paid for the use of their names. However, they seem to be unable to name famous writers who graduated from their courses and went on to success. Twenty years ago, a survey among well-known writers showed that none had taken correspondence courses.

Do your own survey. Check out the books by your favorite authors. Usually there's a capsule biography, giving the author's background, on the book jacket. Spend a few hours in a bookstore or library trying to find one who graduated from a correspondence course.

The Myth That it's Easy

It's not. It's unusually difficult. The main reason is that writing is an over-crowded field. It's harder today because many people have computers with word processing programs, and some of them are trying their hand at writing. This means that most aspiring writers will inevitably be left out in the cold. There isn't enough room for all of them.

It's far more difficult to become a writer than the purveyors of any quickie course admit. Learning the basic knowledge is only the first step. Some aspects, such as the creativity to write fiction that sells, is something that you can never learn. You either have it or you don't.

As you enter the writing field, you'll find the competition fierce. You'll have to hustle to make yourself known, with no guarantee of success. When you become known and established, there will be a flood of newcomers trying to edge you out, as you did to the established writers when you were new to the field.

The Myth of the SASE

Some advise that you send a self-addressed, stamped envelope (SASE) with each query and manuscript. This is something you'll see in every book aimed at aspiring writers, yet it's mostly false. Let's look at some hard facts, which you'll find to be true when you start sending out queries.

Many editors will reply whether you include an SASE or not. The publisher has plenty of stamps and envelopes. Some editors will reply, but on their own letterhead. They'll discard your envelope. Some editors simply won't reply to you, no matter how many SASE's you include. Perhaps they already have enough writers, or don't have the time to reply, or are simply rude people.

With modern e-mail, and electronic submissions, the SASE is rapidly becoming obsolete. We'll go into depth concerning this in the chapter on word processors.

You can waste a lot of money by sending SASE's out needlessly. We'll look very closely at the question of when and to whom you should send an SASE.

The Myth of Glamorizing Fiction and Poetry

The practical reality is that fiction is very "iffy." Poetry is practically hopeless. Poets usually have to pay to get published. Ads seeking poets appear in writer's magazines. The typical arrangement is that, in return for inclusion, the poet agrees to buy a certain number of books. In effect, he co-publishes in company with the other poets.

The Myth of "Writer's Block"

This topic gets much more attention than it deserves because of the mystery surrounding it. What is "writer's block," anyway?

This is a layman's corruption of a term borrowed from psychoanalysis. A "block" means an interruption of memory for unconscious reasons. Supposedly, writers are susceptible to this, at times unable to put a single word onto paper because of this "block."

"Writer's block" is often a convenient excuse for goofing off. Writers get lazy, as do other people. They sometimes need their crutches and self-justifications.

"Writer's block," if it occurs at all, is very rare. In reality, "diarrhea of the keyboard" is far more common. This happens when a writer becomes intoxicated with his own prose, and takes a paragraph to express what should take only a sentence. It's very common, and is an annoyance to an editor who wants a concise manuscript for an article and instead gets a book.

It's extremely difficult for a writer to go over his own work and cut judiciously, removing excess words without impairing the meaning. Some can't do it, or lose the ability to do so with success. More than one excellent novelist has produced increasingly lengthy and turgid books as his career progressed and he found that he could sell books on the strength of his name alone.

It's important to assess your prospects for writing with cold-hearted realism. Viewing the writer's world with rose-colored glasses can only lead to disillusionment and disappointment. Instead, look at it the way it is, not as the myth-makers portray it.

Notes:

1. This happened once to the author. I'd sent in an article, and got it back with a rejection slip a few weeks later. The week after that, I saw the latest issue of the magazine, with an article written by the editor. It was on the same topic as mine, covered the same points, and had similar photographs. The message was clear. The editor had decided that he'd do the article himself. He paraphrased my article, and took his own photographs to illustrate it. It was pointless to protest, as I had no legal recourse that was practical. It doesn't pay to sue for only a few hundred dollars.

Chapter Three
Getting Started

Begin by asking yourself a couple of tough questions:

What do you want to write about?

Are you qualified?

Be realistic about your writing and the potential market. Do you want to write fiction? Poetry? Non-fiction? Maybe you wrote in college or high school, but was it for a paying market, or the school publication? You need to ask yourself some tough questions to avoid making a false start.

Check out the market, and look at what's currently being published in the field you select. Ask yourself, and answer honestly, "Could I write as well as that?" Perhaps you can. You may even be able to write better. If so, you've got a chance.

What talent do you need to earn a living as a writer? The answer depends on what sort of writing you wish to do. If your ambition is to be a technical writer, for example, employed by a manufacturer to write specifications and instruction booklets, you need to understand your language and be able to put words and sentences together coherently. You also need to understand the equipment you'll be describing well enough to write about it. A moderate technical vocabulary is essential.

Most people think of a writer as being a freelancer, though, and this is the sort upon which we'll concentrate our attention in this book. To be a freelancer, you need everything a technical writer needs, plus a few more qualities. Your knowledge of your language must be somewhat better than that of the technical writer. You won't be writing manuals, but books and articles that must sell on their own merits.

Luck

Let's also discuss briefly one other quality you need, and without which you won't get anywhere — luck. Luck is supremely important. You need luck to make the right connections at the right times. Because of this, luck is at least as important as anything else, even though people's perceptions of the importance of luck are often distorted because, for most people, luck tends to "average out." Those few who are very lucky are not likely to ascribe their successes to luck. It's much more flattering to take full credit, and to claim that sheer ability and willpower did the trick.

We find this especially in the writing field. Because writing is intellectual, and writers are generally proud of what they do, we'll find a severe distortion of reality when reading about writers, especially if they're writing autobiographical pieces.

From time to time, a famous writer will be asked to do an article describing "how he did it" for a writer's magazine. Obviously, if he writes that it was mainly luck, there would be no appeal. To sell the article, he has to follow the "party line," and describe how he did it with his massive intellect, his skillful choice of words, and his unequaled plot laying skill. In reality, luck helps in making contacts and placing manuscripts. A writer can send an excellent manuscript to an editor, but if a similarly excellent one on the same topic arrived the week before, the writer's out of luck.

Writer's magazines and writing schools ignore luck. They prefer to tell the aspiring writer that he needs them to help him succeed. Admitting that luck plays any more than an insignificant part is like admitting that they don't have much to sell.

Schools for Writers

There are many credulous people in this world, and skillful liars know that the most successful lies are those that tell the victim what he wants to hear. Politicians do it all the time. Other people who get away with flagrant lies year after year are the operators of writer's schools.

The story that these people tell is that a beginner needs simply to take a correspondence course from them to learn how to achieve success. The ads promise instructions and guidance by experienced professional writers, which leads to earning a lot of money with relatively little effort. They adroitly avoid the question of why, if their instructors are truly skilled writers, they're not earning their living by writing instead of wasting their time teaching. Teaching is a poorly paid occupation, and any writer worth his salt will be working as a writer, not an instructor.

Writer's schools, especially the correspondence schools, are total wastes of money. The impersonal instruction is uninspiring. The student gets a series of stereotyped lessons, rehashing what he could have learned in high school and college, and he gets to submit "assignments" for "review." Let's note one important fact about what happens to these assignments. They're definitely not read by any of the famous authors mentioned in the school's literature. They're gone over by tired, overworked, and underpaid "instructors" who are probably students working their way through college.

The only education worth getting to start off a career in writing is basic language: spelling, grammar, and syntax. This is available in high school for the eager student. It's possible to pick up a refresher course in college, and even one on "writing style." However, note that developing a "style" is much simpler than many of these purveyors of advanced education admit.

One aspect of paying for these courses that doesn't appear in the ads is that often the student must sign a third-party contract, promising to pay a bank or finance company monthly payments to "pay off" the tuition, which the school receives up front.

Phasing Into Writing

The worst thing you can do, unless you're unusually lucky or just plain wealthy, is to sit down one day and say, "I'm going to be a writer." Be honest with yourself. A few people do this as "ego-tripping." Are you on an ego-trip? If you quit your job, you'll have a hard time making it, because there's practically always a gap, usually many months, between doing the work and getting paid for it. As we'll see, it takes time to be recognized. As we've seen in earlier pages, it's best to go slowly, and get into writing step by step.

Emotional Stamina

Do you have the emotional stamina for writing? Writing is a high-pressure, but low-key occupation. There's a lot of pressure on you to bring in the dollars, but practically nobody ever screams at you as in certain other occupations. You don't have anyone standing over you, watching your every move. The lack of face-to-face contact is an advantage, in the sense that it tends to reduce the pressure on you, but it can seem lonely, too.

Emotional stamina also means withstanding the negative effects of rejections. Many people, understandably, are sensitive to rejection because it undermines their self-worth. This is one of those topics we just don't discuss for the most part. It is emotionally trying and ego-battering to suffer rejection, whether personally or professionally. Some people can take it, while others can't without serious effects.

Equipment You'll Need

Fortunately, the equipment needed to start writing is minimal. A typewriter is one basic tool. Nobody accepts handwritten manuscripts. However, today a typewriter is obsolete unless you're living under very primitive conditions. A computer is the more likely choice.

Is it essential to learn touch-typing? Not necessarily. Some very successful writers have never learned touch-typing. They are very fast with the hunt-and-peck method.[1] We'll get further into typewriters and other equipment in a later chapter.

Waiting for the "First Break"

This can be a trying time. Approaching an editor without having been previously published can be anxiety-provoking. Don't let it bother you too much. Every writer has been through this. Editors are also on the lookout for new talent. While to the aspiring writer it may seem that all editors ever do is find reasons to reject queries and manuscripts, many of them dream of being the one to discover a new Zane Grey or James Michener.

Starting Strategy

Be aware that the big-name magazines are not the best places to start. First, they don't always pay top dollar. Some of them are quite miserly. Another point is that they're deluged with manuscripts; the competition is stiff, especially from beginners who want to start at the top. Often, they publish a disappointingly small ratio of entries, such as 1 in 100, or in 1,000.

At the outset, you'll find it difficult to keep going if you're not immediately accepted. It can be very trying if your first few rejections are from that minority of editors who seem to go out of their way to be nasty, and produce rejection letters like this gem:

"Yawn. We have enough of that material already."

Or this:

"What makes you think you're an authority on that subject?"

If at first you don't succeed with one editor, DON'T try, try again with the same manuscript. If your first try with him fails, try again with something different. If that doesn't work, give it one more shot and move on.

Always be prepared to move on to greener pastures, where you'll find an editor who's more receptive. It's also good to keep moving to keep from tiring out an editor. At times, it seems that some editors do become tired of their stable of writers and seek new talent. This is good for the newcomer, but becomes bad news when he's one of the stable.

Diversify. This means striving to get published in as many outlets as you can. There are several good reasons for this, some of which may not be obvious. One reason to diversify is that having a number of outlets avoids giving a particular editor the power of life and death over your income. If you choose to sell to only one outlet you risk becoming a captive, and you will once again be working for a boss.

Some of your accounts will die. This is inevitable. Publishers fail, merge, or disappear for other reasons. The only questions are when and how many. You need to insure yourself against this shutting down of outlets by developing more clients.

Spreading yourself around also shows editors that you're being published in other outlets, too. Knowing that others are willing to pay you to write for them boosts your value in the marketplace.

You'll also be able to compare different editors and how they treat you. Inevitably, you'll find that some treat you better than others do. Some pay better. Others publish your work faster. Some are difficult personalities, and others are enjoyable to work with.

Now let's look at various aspects of writing in detail, because you'll need to give them close study. In the following chapters, you'll find some unexpected problems, and ways of working through and around them that they don't teach you in school.

Notes:

1. Myself included. I've always been a lousy typist.

Chapter Four
Seeking a Market

What market do you wish to enter? How do you approach it? Will they accept you? These are anxiety-provoking questions for the beginner.

The fear of rejection is real. This is what stalls many aspirants. A good way to cope with this fear is to have solid knowledge of the market and what it demands. This forms a basis for acquiring the rest of what you need to know to make your entry. It allows you to make an intelligent choice regarding which markets to try.

Knowing the market is essential, and you'll see this advice in many texts. Unfortunately, few explain exactly what this means. Let's get into it and deal precisely with what you need to know about a possible market.

The first step is to know the publishing house and its policies. There are several elementary steps you need to take to accomplish this. The best way is to look over what it publishes. This is very simple, and in fact is so simple that it's easy to overlook.

The main reason for doing this is to determine if you can provide the sort of material that the publishing house uses. You would not, for example, write an article on birth control for a publisher specializing in certain religious books or magazines. You might also find that a publishing house uses several different types of materials. A large magazine publisher, for example, usually puts out a variety of magazines covering many different topics, such as hot rods, motorcycles, camping, and hunting. Book publishers also may specialize, or may have different divisions catering to different markets. A small publishing house may, for example, specialize in health topics; another, only in those that come under the heading of "outdoor life." Huge publishers, such as Macmillan and Prentice-Hall, serve different markets such as schoolbooks and professional texts. They have entirely separate divisions for their different markets, and for practical purposes you'd better consider each division as a separate company.

Sources of information are easy to acquire. One way to find out about a market is to go to the newsstand or the local library. Another is to send for the publisher's catalog.

The most valuable source of information for its size is the "writer's guidelines" many publishers put out. This is usually a one-page summary of editorial policies and practices. Generally, it lists the type of material the editor seeks, the length of the manuscripts needed, the types of photographs or artwork to accompany the manuscript, and other relevant details. Often the guidelines will include the range of payments, and the method of payment, whether on acceptance, publication, etc.

Not all publishing houses put out writer's guidelines. This may seem surprising, but it's true. Some of the largest publishers don't do it. Some say that they simply can't be bothered. Others are too small to justify it, according to what they say. This is unprofessional, but it's the real world.

It's important to compare the writer's guidelines with what actually appears in the publications. Some of the information listed in the guidelines may be inaccurate. For example, almost all published guidelines specify the lengths of manuscripts wanted, but a look at the publisher's output usually shows that articles and books vary in length, as well as format.

Writer's guidelines may be obsolete. Sometimes new editors compose new guidelines upon assuming the job, but many simply let it ride, because of inertia, laziness, or simply pressure of events. In any event, we'll discuss writer's guidelines in detail in the next chapter.

A quick initial survey can tell you most of what you need to know. Reading the publications you're considering helps a lot, in the sense that it tells you many facets often not covered in the guidelines. Reading the text tells you about the style actually published. Is it serious, academic, humorous, or what? You will often find that you have to tailor your style to suit the publisher's preferences.

You can also find out about the competition you face. In this regard, there can be misleading signals. If the quality of the material is high, you may be misled into thinking that you can't compete, and therefore should not even try. This is not necessarily so. The publisher may simply have high standards, and that does not preclude your attempting to gain acceptance.

You may have to be careful when the material is of poor quality, and you're tempted to tell yourself, "I can do better than this garbage." You probably can, but before starting, ask yourself why the publication includes what you consider to be garbage. It may be that the editor can't tell good material from bad. It also may be that the author is a friend of the editor or publisher, in which case you and other new authors may be locked out. You'll find nepotism and cliques in publishing, as in any other field, and if you try to break in, you're playing against a stacked deck.

The first time you approach a publisher can be important. The real reason for this is that it will have a greater effect on you than on the editor or publisher. A rejection may discourage you from trying again. On the other hand, editors throw queries into the circular file every day, and tend to forget the ones they discard. If you submit a query that's rejected or unanswered, you can be sure that the editor won't hold it against you. You have good reason to try again if you feel you have something else that stands a chance of acceptance.

To whom do you write? This can be puzzling, because whatever the titles listed on the masthead, the relationships and division of labor in each editorial office will vary. A rule of thumb is to start at the top. Write to the "editor-in-chief" or the "editorial director" and wait to see who answers you.

Some top editors make it a point never to deal directly with an author, and always delegate correspondence to a subordinate. No matter how often you try, you'll never get an answer from them. In such cases, resign yourself to dealing with an intermediary, and be as polite with the subordinate as you would be with the top editor. This is important, because you need the intermediary's good will.

Other editors make it a point to deal personally with all or most of their authors. The pressure of work makes delegating some of the work inevitable. Some editors will contact authors whose work they want to accept, and leave to a subordinate the routine task of writing and addressing rejection letters.

Introducing yourself to a new publication is important. It's also difficult. If you're a previously published author, you already have a foot in the door. Be sure to include a list of your previous publications. If you suspect that the editor may not even have heard of you, you may wish to include photocopies of a couple of articles. A good tactic is to make the introductory letter serve double duty by including a query.

Here's the way an introductory letter might read:

date

company
address
attention: Robert Blank, Editor-in-Chief

Dear Mr. Blank,

I'd like to write for your publication. My expertise in the field includes (list your special knowledge). You will find enclosed a list of my recent publications for your review. Also enclosed is an outline of an article (book) I'd appreciate your considering.

I'd appreciate your sending me a copy of your writer's guidelines. For your convenience I have enclosed a self-addressed, stamped envelope.

If you have any questions, please feel free to contact me.

Thank you for your cooperation.

Yours truly,

your name
your address
your phone number

If you're not a previously published author, you have to concentrate on selling the subject, not yourself. Your letter then might read like this:

date

company
address
attention: Robert Blank, Editor-in-Chief

Dear Mr. Blank,
    I'd like to write for your publication. Your company specializes in (list the field) and I have special knowledge that would make an interesting article (book). I have enclosed an outline for your consideration. Also enclosed is the first three pages of my projected article (book), so that you can see my writing style.
    I'd appreciate your sending me a copy of your writer's guidelines. For your convenience I have enclosed a self-addressed, stamped envelope.
    If you have any questions, please feel free to contact me. Thank you for your time.

Yours truly,

your name
your address
your phone number

Avoid flowery language and avoid wasting words in your letters. Editors get many letters, and they haven't got the time to wade through huge texts. State briefly what you have to say and then end it! Editors appreciate people who avoid wasting their time.

Be sure to list exactly what you can do for the editor in a first-time query. One important point with many editors is whether or not the author can include high-quality photographs. If you can take and print your own photos, be sure to mention this. Better yet, include a sample print. Some publications, as a matter of policy, will not accept submissions that don't include photographs.

Observing the formalities and including an SASE can't do any harm, and it's the safest course with the first submission. You'll gradually see what the situation will allow, and most likely you'll be able to dispense with SASEs altogether with most of your outlets, especially if they accept electronic submissions. In any event, sending a SASE with your first manuscript or two should not be a serious problem. If the editor later occasionally rejects one, he'll surely pay the postage to return your manuscript. With modern computers and digital photography, the cost of postage on a SASE is more than the cost of the paper and disc. If the editor rejects most or all of them, it's time to try another outlet.

Today, most editors have e-mail addresses, and it's becoming customary to submit a query via e-mail. This saves you both time and postage. Often, you can expect an e-mail reply within a day or two.

The telephone can help you get a quick answer to a query, but there are very few situations that justify this speed. The simple, hard fact is that most situations aren't urgent, and treating them as if they are will only waste your money. Editors do not accept collect calls, which means that you have to pay the bill. Using the phone is expensive, especially when the person you want isn't in, or perhaps is in a meeting and cannot be disturbed.

Another reason to avoid phoning is that some editors are truly disturbed by telephone calls. These are interruptions in their workdays, and they resent them. They may go so far as to instruct their staffs to tell callers that they're not in.

A phone commitment is usually risky. People tend to forget what they say, and often you can be left holding the bag

An editor can make a commitment in good faith, but can also forget, or assign the same article twice. Then there are a few editors who will not make written commitments. They will give their verbal approval only. Possibly it's because of a reluctance to make a promise on paper. Also, they may dislike writing letters or e-mails. With these, you'll have to take what you get.

Sometimes, the editor will simply tell you he needs time to think it over, or will ask you to send him a fully worked out proposal in writing. There are some who don't want to make snap decisions, and will always play for time this way. It's vital for you to understand that you can't push an editor. He'll make his decision in his own good time, and you must be patient.

Don't make the mistake of thinking that high-pressure tactics will work. Telling an editor that you have someone else considering the manuscript right now will not impress him greatly. Editors don't like to be manipulated and resent this sort of treatment. There are some "success stories" in the trade about some individuals who were able to use such door kicking tactics successfully, and if you think you can get the same results, go ahead and good luck. Be prudent, though, and wait until you're well known and in great demand before you try to bully an editor.

How long should you wait for an answer? Thirty days is about right for a snail mail query, and much less for e-mail. Most editors will reply in these time frames, if they're going to reply at all. If you're trying a new publication, you might mail a reminder after thirty days, but don't place much hope in it.

An editor who doesn't have the consideration to reply within a reasonable time isn't worth it, and you'll lose more than you gain in trying to deal with him. A polite "I thought you weren't interested when you didn't reply" will get the point across.

A vital question is: "How long should you let an editor hold on to your material without replying?" Thirty to sixty days is about right. If he can't make up his mind in that time, you may consider seeking another outlet.

One fact you have to face is that material can grow stale. If, for example, you're planning a Christmas article or piece of fiction, you have to get it sold within a certain time or wait until next year. If your field is car testing, for example, no editor will be interested in last year's model.

How many times should you try before giving up? The answer to this question is very important, and you must balance the negative and discouraging effects of being rejected against your realistic appraisal of the market. It's vital to avoid becoming discouraged. There are many possible reasons why you're being rejected or ignored, and not all of them reflect badly on you. Editors usually don't give reasons. They don't have to. Also, they want to avoid unproductive discussions with authors or potential authors. They don't have the time to spend in exchanging letters with many authors, giving them advice on how to "make it" for their publications.

Be realistic. If you find yourself with three rejections in a row, try another publisher. There are many publishers out there, and it's bad strategy trying to break down a door that remains closed to you.

One point to watch is simultaneous queries or submissions. This can place you in an awkward position. Getting the go-ahead from two publications for the same piece means that you have to choose, which is often not difficult. It's not likely that two editors will reply at the same time. If one gives you the go-ahead, and you receive a go-ahead from another editor later, reply that you'd thought he wasn't interested when you hadn't heard from him, and that you'd queried another publication.

There are several types of assignments. The most common type is to do a piece "on speculation." This is what many authors, even experienced and established ones, have to face. It's the cruelest part of the way editors treat writers. What this means in plain language is: "You do the work, all of the running around, do the writing, shoot the photos, and send the results to me. I'll look at it, and if I like it, maybe I'll publish it when I'm good and ready."

The policy of handing out assignments and accepting articles on speculation is often disguised by euphemisms. Letters that say, "I'll be happy to review the article," or some such language, are simply telling you to do it on speculation. The editor commits himself only to "review" it, without promising even how long it'll take him to do so.

Some established, well-known authors can get assignments that are more definite. In some instances, the publisher will even pay expenses incurred. If the assignment is definite, there's usually some sort of guarantee stated or implied. Some publishers will pay a "kill fee" for material they decide not to use.

You'll have to feel out your market. An editor may never make a commitment, but if he accepts nine out of ten of your submissions, it's worth continuing with him. On the other hand, some editors will commit to almost anything, then bounce most of the articles back at you.

It's worthwhile, at this point, to consider some of the reasons an article or piece of fiction might be rejected. It might simply not work out the way the editor had expected. The editor might have had a preconceived idea that he failed to communicate to the author. The author, not knowing, might have placed the wrong "slant" on the piece. Another reason might be that the editor has just published a similar piece, and feels that he has no room for more for a while. Yet another might be a directive from above — "No more articles on bloodshot eyes for at least a year!"

For beginners, the most anxious period comes after mailing off the first submission. Waiting for a reply can be nerve-wracking. It's important to resist the temptation to "bug" an editor for a reply. Usually, they're fairly quick about this, especially if the verdict is a rejection. They'll want to ship it back to the author as quickly as possible to clear their desks.

At this point, let's note that some editors are so disorganized that everything you send them disappears into a black hole, to reappear upon publication. If this sort of editor treats you fairly, and publishes everything he doesn't lose, it may be worth continuing with him, accepting the loss of a small percentage of your articles.

It's best when the publisher provides written contracts to authors. Signing a contract lays out the terms exactly, and tends to protect everyone's interests better than most unwritten understandings. The kill fee, if any, may be listed. The time limit, if the publisher accepts one, may also be listed. A publisher who does not provide written contracts can be tricky at times, although not necessarily because of an intent to deceive. It can happen that an author genuinely misunderstands what the publisher accepts as common practice.

Do Your Homework. This is the central point of this chapter. If you are diligent, and do your homework, you'll have no guarantee of success, but you'll have an edge that certain of your competitors will lack. You'll be able to plan a systematic campaign to get published and to keep getting published, while less careful workers will be haphazard and depend more on pure luck.

Chapter Five
Understanding Writer's Guidelines

Sending a manuscript "cold" to a publisher is a serious mistake for a writer unless he is so well known that editors almost always accept his work. It's a waste of postage, especially for a beginner, because the chances of getting it accepted are so remote that it's not worth the effort.

Strangely, a few publications suggest sending the entire manuscript "cold," instead of a query. These are the ones with little regard for their writers. Their viewpoint is truly: "You do all the work, all the writing and research, and we'll take a look at it, and maybe we'll buy it if we feel like it." It's best to avoid these publishers, because you're playing against a stacked deck.

Instead, it's preferable to understand your market, and make contact with a publisher before writing anything for him. Here's why:

To succeed, you need accurate information. This advice seems stale and unoriginal, and it is. The problem is that many people neither understand nor accept it. It's vital that you know what sort of material your potential customer wants. There are two steps to finding out what your potential outlet's needs are.

The first is to scan several of his publications. If it's a magazine, look at several issues. If your prospect is a book publisher, look at several books he's published and then look carefully at his catalog. You may want to work it the other way: look at his catalog, select several books that interest you, and read them. You may be surprised to find out that you already subscribe to the magazine for which you'd like to write. The odds are overwhelming that you're interested in writing about a familiar field. If so, you probably subscribe to a related magazine or two, or have a number of books on the subject. It's obvious that you should select a field that you know. Try to write from total ignorance and you'll crash and burn.

Next, write an introductory letter and ask for a copy of the writer's guidelines. Surprisingly, some major publishers don't even have writer's guidelines. That's very unprofessional, but that's life. If you come across one that doesn't, there are general guidelines that you can use. It's not too hard to understand that a manuscript should follow a standard format, and be neat. It's also easy to learn what length articles they publish from scanning an issue of a magazine and noting the average article or story length.

Let's look at a set of typical writer's guidelines and see what we can derive. Don't expect too much, because sometimes writer's guidelines don't tell you much that you don't already know:

ABC PUBLISHING, INC.
Editorial Guidelines

ABC Magazine is a high-quality publication with high standards. We accept only the highest quality and professional manuscripts.

This introduction is pure puffery, and the result of the editor's ego-tripping. Ignore it, and go on to the next paragraph, which is more relevant.

Manuscripts should be typed, double-spaced, and on only one side of the sheet of paper. Do not staple pages together. Paper clips are acceptable. Only original typed manuscripts are acceptable. Carbon or photocopies are not. No dot matrix submissions accepted. The author's name, address, telephone, and Social Security number should be typed in the upper left corner of the first page, and the author's name, article title, and page number should be at the top of every page. The article should begin halfway down the first page.

This is understandable, but hardly tells you anything about the particular market. These are general and common sense guidelines, and probably the only reason for their inclusion is that there are some newcomers out there who don't know what form a manuscript should take.

There are some other points to watch, and often these are not listed in the guidelines.

A neat manuscript is extremely important. This is both your product and your selling tool. A neat query, which is purely a selling tool, is also important, but not quite as much as the manuscript.

The first basic principle is to give the editor what he wants. This is probably the most common reason for rejection of a manuscript. This means following the guidelines closely and meticulously. It also means following any special instructions the editor has for you.

Let's lay out the typical manuscript format, and examine the details of producing it:

Your Name
Your Address
Your City, State, ZIP
Your Phone Number
Your Social Security number

TITLE
Your Name or Pen Name

Text

----

etc.

The title should be about halfway down the page, and the text begins right under the title. Every page should be numbered, preferably with a "header." The header can be the title and page number, but if you want to be fancy, you can have your name, the title, and the page number, in that order.

The paper should be 8½″ x 11″ white paper, simply because this is what most editors specify. Occasionally, you may find an editor who will accept, and even prefer, off-white paper because it reduces glare. Always ask before submitting any manuscript on anything but standard white paper. Don't worry if the writer's guidelines specify "bond" paper, don't even worry about what the term means. Most editors themselves don't know. White typing paper, 20-pound or heavier, is perfectly adequate.

The term, "20-pound," refers to the weight, or thickness of the paper. You may prefer 13-pound to save a bit on postage, but whatever you do, don't use any very thin paper, onionskin, or any paper that looks "chintzy."

Manuscripts should be double-spaced. Some editors call for triple-spaced manuscripts, but they're very rare. Your name, address, telephone number, and Social Security number should be at the upper left corner of the first page. The text should begin about halfway down the page. Your name, or whichever pen name you're using, should be right above it. See the example already given.

Neatness counts. Some manuscripts are sloppy, with XXX'd out words and pencil corrections. Many editors are turned off by obviously sloppy work, and feel that this shows a severe lack of craftsmanship and professionalism. You won't find this in many guidelines, but it's nonetheless true. Producing a neat manuscript is no problem with today's computers and printers.

In this regard, it's a good idea to go over the text several times to correct spelling errors and typographical errors, called "typos" for short. Too many errors mean too much work for an editor, and could cause your manuscript to be rejected.

Don't, however, make the mistake of being a perfectionist. Try not to submit a perfect manuscript. Strangely, this can turn off some editors. Editors like to think that they're smarter than their authors, and an author who sends in excruciatingly correct manuscripts may antagonize the occasional perverse editor. It does no harm to leave one or two typos in the manuscript, as this gives the editor something to edit, and feeds his ego.

An indication of this type of editor is the change for change's sake, and this editor will find reason to paraphrase some of your sentences. You can submit a perfect manuscript, correct in every way, and still find some revisions inserted by an editor who found something not to his liking.

As noted in the guidelines cited, each page should have a heading. The heading should be your name, the title, and the page number. It occasionally happens that an editor will clumsily knock a pile of papers off his desk, or fumble a manuscript. Having the proper call out on each page makes reassembling manuscripts easier when this happens.

Let's continue with our set of guidelines:

Articles should be between 2000 and 3000 words long. While shorter articles are acceptable, longer ones require too much editing and are generally not as desirable. Photos should accompany every article, and should be keyed to captions. We accept only black & white photographs, 5 x 7 or larger. Captions preferably should be longer than absolutely required, as we can cut these down if necessary. A model release is required for each person appearing in the photographs.

This paragraph tells you more about the publication's needs. The article length is important, especially because many writers tend to overdo it instead of being concise. Remember the myth about "writer's block?"

The information on photographs is important, and any author should note the specified print size carefully. There's no technical reason why a high-quality print of smaller size can't do for publication, but editors want authors to follow their instructions. The point regarding a model release is worth noting, but if you use photographs with your material, you should obtain model releases just on general principles. In practice, however, publications rarely ask to see any model releases. It's impractical for them to try to verify that the people who appear in the photographs are actually the ones who signed the model releases.

No previously published material is acceptable. Simultaneous submissions are also not acceptable. All material is submitted on speculation only. Payment is upon publication.

This is the hard line. Read this carefully, and decide whether or not you can live with it. Many publications will not accept "seconds," that have been published elsewhere. This is their right. Some editors make a major point of this, and avow that any writer whom they catch sending them a "second" will never write for them again.

The part regarding simultaneous submissions is a useless stipulation. There's no practical way for an editor to even know that you're submitting anything to anyone else, especially if you use a pen name. A problem can come if two publications accept your piece. If an editor sees an article with the same wording in another publication, the pen name won't fool him. Some editors are so touchy that they will resent your writing another article on the same topic, even if it's totally different and has a different focus.

The sentence regarding "speculation" is worth remembering, because it's basically a disclaimer of responsibility. It may or may not be a serious obstacle, depending on the people involved. Some editors include this sentence in their guidelines just to give them an "out" in case someone sends in a manuscript that's pure junk. Others seem to make it a practice to reject articles because they can't make up their minds on the basis of a query.

The sentence describing the method of payment is also vitally interesting, because it tells you when you'll get paid. It can mean a long delay, depending on the publication, before you see any money. The guidelines may or may not state how much the publisher will pay. If there's mention of payment, it will usually give a range, rather than a single figure.

Some guidelines call for a covering sheet, or "routing sheet," which is a form that the author fills out, and which gives the title, word length, and other information about the submission. The publication may also require a signed statement that the author has not plagiarized the work, nor submitted it to any other publication. This is almost always included in any contract the publication requires you to sign before acceptance.

An important point to watch today relates to electronic submissions. The editor may require a disk containing the text to accompany the manuscript. Take careful note of the type of disc required, so that you can give the editor what he wants. Also, always send "hard copy," the printed manuscript, along with the disk, unless the editor requests that you send your manuscript via e-mail for speed.

It's worth the trouble to look over the guidelines once more before mailing in a submission. A quick look before sealing the envelope can't do any harm, and can prevent a serious error. Guidelines vary from editor to editor, and it's quite true that one man's meat is another's poison.

Chapter Six
Editors

Making a success of writing centers around the problem of approaching editors and persuading them to accept you and your work. Although the readers are the ultimate customers, the editors are the ones you must "sell." This is why we'll spend a lot of time examining editors, their situations, and their problems, in an effort to understand the way they think.

It's crucial to understand an important and fundamental fact about the writer's market — it's an overcrowded market. This is a theme that you'll see running constantly through this study because it dominates the picture. There are too many writers for the markets available, and the competition is fierce. This makes it a "buyer's market." This is what stacks the deck against you. Editors can pick and choose among many, many writers, knowing that if one proves unsatisfactory for any reason, there are several others waiting to take his place.

Editors work in a myth-making environment. Many writers hold them in awe because of the editors' almost god-like power to accept or reject a writer's efforts. Sometimes this becomes ridiculous, as when a well-known writer "dedicates" one of his books to his editor with an adulatory paragraph that exaggerates the editor's virtues. Let's look at one composite example:

> *"This book is affectionately dedicated to John Grouch, editor extraordinaire, whose acumen and insight made a better writer of me."*

This is the sort of self-serving compliment by a writer about an editor who helped him. Always take these with a grain of salt. They may be true. They also may be simple and cheap investments in the writer's future. We also find this sort of exaggerated flattery when certain writers accept literary prizes. This is a good time to "stroke" an editor and attribute the writer's success to him. Editors want recognition too, and they're as susceptible to flattery as are other people. Some writers take full advantage of this. In other instances, editors will subtly demand flattery, and cut off any writer who does not provide it.

This is why you need to "stroke" an editor. This goes beyond the principle that a few kind words can't do any harm. Many editors need their egos fed. Read the publication. If it's on a topic that interests you (and it damn well should be, if you're going to write about it) you will often find an article you like especially well. A note to the editor can't do any harm. A compliment for the article also compliments the editor's judgment in selecting that article for publication. Don't overdo it, though. Don't get sickeningly sweet or too lavish in your praise. Don't write as if the person deserves the Nobel Prize. Editors aren't stupid, and they sooner or later will spot obvious insincerity.

Editors Have Bosses, Too

Another, and equally important, point about "stroking" editors is that some of them catch hell from the boss, the publisher. As in other occupations, sometimes the boss is a petty, mean, tyrannical type who makes his employees' lives hell. An editor whose ego takes a beating from his boss can use a few strokes.

One tight-fisted publisher made life hell for the fifteen editors who worked for him. The firm put out fifteen publications on topics ranging from motorcycles to hot-rods to survival. Unfortunately, when the time came for new equipment, the publisher would price-shop, buying the cheapest available, without regard to its suitability for the task. The editors would have to work with what the publisher had bought, which usually turned out to be temperamental and unreliable. Although the frequent equipment breakdowns often delayed the work, the publisher still held the editors responsible for getting their respective publications out on time.

Another publisher, an innovator with a very successful magazine he'd built from scratch, developed a bad name in the industry because he went through editors as if they were paper towels. He also mistreated individual employees and practiced what is known today as "sexual harassment" with female staff. As one of his former employees said: "The magazine publishing business, magazines, newspapers, and/or books, is much the same as any other production industry — it takes all kinds."

The Editor's Workday

Editors don't spend their entire days reading manuscripts. Indeed, contrary to some impressions, they do relatively little reading of the mass of material they face each day. They can't. There aren't enough hours in the day.

The hard fact is that almost everyone who thinks he or she can write will send queries or manuscripts. Some are so ineptly done that the editor can see by the first paragraph that there's no hope for it. This is the category of manuscript or query that will get the quick treatment, and a reply only if the sender has provided a self-addressed envelope.

Many other manuscripts are as easy for the editor to categorize. Some are well done, but deal with a topic that the editor doesn't wish to cover. Others may deal with something already slated for the next issue, in which case the editor simply won't read it, but will summarily return it.

The only instances in which an editor will read the manuscript completely are those resulting from assignments, and those dealing with a topic he wants to cover soon. The editor simply doesn't have enough time to read other manuscripts no matter how well written.

Editors can't spend much time reading manuscripts because they have other duties. One is to lay out the next issue of the magazine. A book editor often has to work with a designer deciding the layout of a new book. The routine work of laying out a publication is demanding. Generally, the editor starts with a "dummy," sent over from the advertising department. The dummy shows the positioning of the ads, and the editor's task is to lay his articles into the unoccupied spaces. Every magazine is built around its ads. This requires using judgment in selecting articles and placing their components around the ads. Sometimes it's necessary to cut an article to make it fit. This is where photographs help the editor, because a photograph provides great flexibility. He can enlarge or reduce the photograph to fit the available space. If the article comes with a number of photographs, he can use the ones he needs to fit the article into the space available.

Each article the editor decides to publish becomes a "custom job." Each one requires typesetting, a decision regarding headline style and size, and careful proofreading. Catching errors is critically important for a number of reasons. One is simply maintaining a good image for the publication. A publication full of spelling errors will not inspire respect among its readers. Another reason has to do with the authors. Whatever the cause, an error in print appears with the author's name attached, and authors aren't thrilled to see an ineptly produced article. Finally, some errors can be very costly. If an article deals with an advertiser's product, a misstatement can alienate him. If it deals with a real person, a wrong word can be libelous and bring a lawsuit.

In principle, layout is simple and straightforward, but the mass of details makes it an uncomfortable task. It becomes especially so if the politics of the company leaves the editor with little power. One practical problem that can arise in magazine layout, for example, is when the advertising department makes a last minute insertion. The layout may be complete, but the new ad will take up some space, obliging the editor to redo one or more pages. Rarely does an editor get full support from top management when he feels that the layout is complete and won't object to the modification. The owner of the company sees the extra ad as extra dollars, and is likely to support the advertising department. In some publishing companies, this is standard practice, and the editor must cope with turmoil until a particular issue is actually on the press. This is one of the stresses some editors face on their jobs.

Every editor faces deadlines. These are dates and times when an issue must be ready to go. An editor who blows too many deadlines will often be looking for another job. In many instances, an editor will have a hard time meeting a deadline. His workday will be interrupted with phone calls, conferences, and the details of supervising his staff. Typically, publishers don't accept excuses from editors. They take the attitude of "If you can't do what I want, I'll find someone who can." This is why editors often stay late at the office. Editors are "salaried," which means they don't get paid overtime, and this puts further stress upon them.

Sometimes an editor can delegate certain tasks to a subordinate. If the subordinate is capable, the editor has only to give the work a once-over before using it. Sometimes, however, a subordinate doesn't understand the task, or the instructions, or may go off on a tangent. This is particularly true of those who are recent graduates, or inexperienced.

A newcomer to the editorial staff, eager to please, may try to impress the editor by exceeding his instructions. If the task is to rewrite and condense an article to fit into a certain slot, the recent graduate may overkill, giving it a total rewrite to show his prowess and consequently totally distorting the perspective of the article.

This touches on one of the problems editors face. They're often not allowed to offer high enough salaries to attract truly adept people, and have to make do with marginally competent assistants. A writer can often get a glimpse of this problem when speaking to the editorial staff on the phone, and finding a new person filling a certain slot each time he calls. Rapid turnover is a tip-off that things are not quite right. When an editor has to get the job done despite lack of ability in the people to whom he'd normally delegate some tasks, he'll try to extend himself to do it. This is what leads to long hours. The quiet evenings are the only periods when the phones stop ringing and the turmoil in the office ceases.

The Editor's "Stable"

Editors typically have a "stable" of writers, regulars who seem to fill most of the pages of every issue. This can be good or bad, depending on your point of view. If you're an outsider trying to break into the market, you may have some unkind thoughts about cliques and how they stack the odds against the honest and aspiring newcomer. If you're part of the stable, you'll find that this provides a certain sense of security.

Let's take a close look at why and how a stable exists. An editor tends to depend on writers who are known quantities, who meet deadlines, and who deliver consistently good work. An editor is reluctant to give an important assignment to a newcomer, because he can't be sure that the newcomer can deliver. In some instances, the editor will have enough "regulars" to fill his needs and will be uninterested in seeking new talent. This is why you'll occasionally find an editor who tells you that he has all the writers he needs.

Editors: The People

Editors like to see themselves as intellectuals of some sort. Editors often have big or tender egos, especially the ones who are failed writers. Another, probably even larger, group is the aspiring writers.

While it's stupid to live by a dictum, occasionally there's a grain of truth in one. The old saying, "Those who can, do. Those who can't, teach," has a nugget of truth in it. It's the same with editors. Why should a talented writer accept most of the editorial jobs, anyway? Long hours, unrelenting pressure, and probably an unappreciative boss are not compelling reasons to take a job.

Why does someone become an editor? Often, it's because he or she can't quite make it as a writer. Sometimes it's simply lack of talent. We must be careful not to ascribe this to too many editors, though. Some are talented writers, but feel that they can't earn a steady living by writing because the market's too crowded. In other instances, a publisher will offer a talented writer a generous salary to be his editor.

Editors Have Other Problems, Too

Low pay is one. Typically, editors feel underpaid for the hours they have to spend working, because they're on salary. We've already seen how low pay affects an editor's ability to recruit competent staff. Pay is also the way the boss expresses his esteem or gratitude for a job well done. A publisher who is parsimonious can only damage his editor's self-esteem and build resentment.

Overwork is another problem. It's easy to become burned out when the hours are long and tiring. Often contributing to the overwork is the flood of queries and manuscripts that arrive. Each requires at least a quick look, and many editors cope with this by delegating the task to a subordinate.

Editors often have strained relationships with their publishers. The editor typically feels that the publisher is a slave driver and expects too much from him. This is why a writer has to be flexible and open-minded in dealing with his market. One who adds to editors' problems will not become very popular.

Deadlines are recurring problems. It seems at times that the publishing industry is filled with gremlins and saboteurs striving to prevent an editor from meeting a deadline. Editors become sensitized to influences that work against a deadline, and tend to focus resentment upon them. An editor usually can't do much if the problem is with the ad department or with the boss, but if he's depending on a writer for an article for a certain issue and the writer's late, he can retaliate.

Another problem for editors can be obtaining payment for writers. Most publications do not pay upon acceptance, but pay when the article appears. Many also pay late. There are reasons for this, one of them being "cash flow." Marginal publications tend to have cash flow problems. Another reason is simple calculation. The publisher reasons that the longer he can keep the money in his bank account, the longer it'll be drawing interest for him. In some instances, this policy can become downright cruel.

One publisher purposely delayed paying writers as long as possible. In one instance, the editor told a writer directly that the head office was delaying payments because the powers-that-be were putting all of their spare cash into T-bills, and paying only writers who complained. Another magazine, an international publication, delayed paying its overseas writers. It's difficult to sue across national boundaries, and when the sum's only a few hundred dollars, it isn't worth it. Editors bear the brunt of complaints from writers for these happenings, and this doesn't make their lives easier.

Understanding the Editor

From this discussion we see that an editor's life has its complications. Some editors cope with these problems very well. Others, facing other problems of varying severity, don't cope well at all.

It's important for you, if you intend to write to sell, to understand what editors face during their working hours. Editors often will not explain all of their reasons and problems to writers, who may blame the editors unjustly for their actions or omissions.

Chapter Seven
How Writers Get Paid

There are basically two ways freelance writers get paid. One is time payments, which we call "royalties." This is often the case with books, where the amount of investment, as well as the returns, can be very high. We'll look at royalties first.

Royalties

A royalty is a percentage of the sale of a book. There are different ways of paying royalties, and the percentage and method of calculation vary with the publisher, as there are no industry-wide standards. The publisher decides upon or negotiates a percentage, which can be from five to twenty-five percent, depending on the individual case and circumstances. The percentage may be based upon the retail price or upon the net price. The usual method is to pay a percentage on the net price, whatever it may be. Publishers have a variety of outlets. Some sell mail order, while others sell through jobbers, distributors, and dealers. The discount off retail price depends upon the quantity. The publisher pays the author his royalties as they accrue. He may calculate and pay them monthly, quarterly, semi-annually, or annually. Publishers prefer to pay royalties on books because their success is uncertain, and paying a writer a percentage of the "take" is

safer than a fixed fee. Established writers can get extra benefits, though.

The publisher may pay an advance on royalties, and deduct the amount of the advance from royalties earned. As
with the percentage and method of calculation, this practice
varies widely with the publisher and the author. Publishers
are less likely to want to take a chance with an unknown author, and this shows itself especially in the payment of advances. An author with a good "track record" stands a better
chance of collecting an advance.

The amount of the advance and the timing of the payment
also vary widely. In the best possible case, a major publishing house will pay a well-known author many thousands of
dollars before the manuscript is finished. This is "front
money" for the author's living expenses, and the publisher
feels confident that it's an investment that will earn him
much more than he lays out. Some companies will pay an
author several payments during the course of the work.
These are "progress payments," usually paid when ordering
technical writing. Other publishing houses pay an advance
upon receipt of the manuscript. Yet others pay no advance at
all.

The advance is just that, basically a loan against royalty
earnings. The author who receives an advance can expect to
see no more money until his work has earned enough to pay
off the amount advanced him. Once his book is "in the
black," he'll continue to receive regular royalty checks until
the book is out of print.

This is one of the strong attractions of the royalty system.
Some books remain in print for years, earning small but
steady incomes for their authors. The writer who specializes
in this type of book is actually making an investment when
he writes, because he will not see all of the benefits immedi-

ately, but will continue to get paid for work completed long ago.

"Best sellers" usually earn a huge amount during their brief terms, then die and vanish into limbo. Some of the better ones become stage or screen plays. The author can earn extra royalties from this. If the author's versatile, he can collect a fee for writing the screenplay. Some best selling authors, such as Evan Hunter and Mario Puzo, are also successful screenwriters.

Can You Trust Your Publisher?

After thinking over this sketch of how the royalty system works, the obvious question that must occur to you relates to the publisher's honesty. How do you know that he's accurately informing you regarding how many books of yours he sells? You don't. You are vulnerable to cheating, if he's so inclined. This isn't a great danger, because most publishers are honest in this regard. There actually have been very few instances of cheating of this sort. Publishers also know that if you became extremely suspicious, and consulted an attorney for advice, they might face having their records subpoenaed and any dishonesty could lead to civil and criminal prosecution. In any event, there are easier ways for a publisher to retain a greater percentage of the "take," legal ones that don't present any danger of prosecution.

For instance, one publisher, who had been paying 15 percent of retail, used this tactic: He simply told the author that the royalties were too high, and that if the author did not sign new contracts which stipulated a 10 percent royalty rate, he'd let the books go out of print. The new contracts also specified that the calculation was to be based on the net price, not retail. The publisher then set his son up in business as a "distributor," and sold all of the books through him. He sold his son the books for 40 percent of retail, the maximum discount. This cut the author's income to one-third of what it had been. Much of the relationship between an author and publisher is based on trust. The author trusts his publisher to play fair. In turn, the publisher trusts the author to be fair with him. He trusts the author not to try to pass off material previously written as new. He also trusts the author to use good judgment and avoid booby-trapping his work with material that might lead to a lawsuit. Plagiarized material can bring a lawsuit. So can anything defamatory. The publisher can usually screen out anything which might bring a libel suit, but unless he's read every book ever written, he can never be sure that one of his authors hasn't picked up some of another's work, trying to pass it off as his own.

Thus, we see that the relationship between author and publisher is a two-way street. Ethics do count. Another consideration is simple self-interest. The publisher knows that if the author suspects that he's not getting a fair deal, he'll go elsewhere with his future works. If the author's reasonably talented, this will deprive the publisher of potential future income.

Purchase of Rights

Outright purchase of rights is the other way to pay an author. Occasionally, a book publisher will pay this way, but only for what he considers a sure success. We find that magazines usually use this method for articles and short stories. Within this category, there are two methods of paying. The first, most desirable for the author, is payment upon acceptance. The publication pays for the piece when the editor decides that he'll use it. This is not, however, the favorite method of payment from the point of view of the businessmen who own the magazines. When the publication pays upon acceptance, it bears the cost of the purchases beyond the cash involved. This ties up the cash with the authors, sometimes months before the pieces appear. Also, articles can go out of date. A biography of a public official who dies or gets impeached, for example, is as dead as yesterday's news. These reasons are why the owners of most magazines prefer to pay upon publication and make the authors wait for their money.

Payment upon publication can impose a hardship for the author. Realistically, many publications have backlogs of a year or more. This dictates that authors usually have to wait a long time for their money. It also forces such publications to accept less than best, because the best don't have to put up with such treatment.

Not surprisingly, those that pay on acceptance are the ones around which writers tend to cluster. It's here that the competition is fiercest. Money does "talk," and such publications can demand, and get, the best talent.

It becomes very difficult for the author when a publisher is late with a payment. The author is in a weak position to demand timely payment because he depends upon the editor's good will for the sale of future articles. Of course, a publisher who's a total deadbeat isn't worth the effort, and his good will is useless. This is when the author must draw the line and decide not to let himself be victimized.

There are other less common types of payments to authors. The "kill fee" is a payment that serves as a sort of consolation prize. Editors may pay this when they decide not to publish an article that they'd previously accepted or had solicited. The kill fee may be a percentage of the fee that the article would have earned, or it may be a fixed sum in every case. Rarely is a kill fee over one hundred dollars. Few publishers pay kill fees. This is mainly because they don't have to. Unless they've signed a contract that specifies a kill fee with the author, they're not obliged to do so. They prefer to let the author take all of the risks.

Some editors will reimburse an author for expenses he incurs in pursuing an article. Expenses may involve taking an interviewee to lunch or there may be minor travel expenses. The author might have to purchase special equipment or supplies, depending on the nature of the article.

As with other payments, the amounts publishers allow vary greatly. Some publications are very generous because the expenses may be much more than the price of the article. When an article requires foreign travel, for example, the fares can easily be several times what the article is worth in cash value. Some publishers set a limit on the amount of expenses they allow authors to charge to them. Others are pretty loose, depending on the author's good judgment not to abuse the privilege. Almost all require documentation by means of receipts, to keep their own bookkeeping straight.

Publishers Who Don't Pay

Occasionally, you'll find an outlet that tries to "stiff" you. This is uncommon, but you may as well prepare yourself to face this at least once during your career. In some instances, such as a publisher who is in the same state, small claims court can provide satisfaction. It's not always practical to sue across state lines, and some small claims courts won't act except on cases within the state. If the publisher is out-of-state, you've simply lost. Hiring a lawyer to try to collect a few hundred dollars is more trouble and expense than it's worth.

One author dealt with such a publisher by writing to say that he was a member of a writer's club, and that he'd mention the incident in the "caution" column in the club publication. This got him immediate payment.

Some authors encounter publications that don't offer payment at all, but expect freebies from authors. These may be professional publications, productions of nonprofit organizations, "house organs," and the like. One such is the *Law Enforcement Bulletin*, published by the Federal Bureau of Investigation. Another is *Security Management*, the house organ of the American Society for Industrial Security.

Should you ever write for free? There are several factors to consider in making the decision.

One is the exposure that the publication affords. In some instances, the publication's very prestigious, and being included in its pages is an honor. In other instances, contributing to the publication can help build contacts needed by an author. It's a good way to meet people and to make a favorable impression.

The other side of this coin is that if it's well-known in the field that the publication doesn't pay, the author may acquire a reputation of being desperate if he has more than an occasional piece included. It's unwise to acquire such a stigma, because this might lead to editors' lowering the value of an author's work, and paying him less.

Another point is that every author sooner or later builds up a file of pieces that have been rejected and that, for various reasons, he can't sell anywhere. These are convenient to use to satisfy a publication requesting freebies.

Yet another consideration is the "fun piece." Almost all authors have certain favorite topics, or pieces they want to write simply for the pleasure. It may be that something needs to be said, or it may be simply entertainment. This is probably a piece that the author hasn't even tried to sell, but one which he can easily write and which he'd like to see in print.

Payment: The Bottom Line

The professional writer lives on the proceeds from his writing. This dictates that he must keep a watchful eye on his income. He must balance the priorities he assigns to his outlets, and give his first attention to those who pay best and soonest.

Part II:
Tools

This part will provide information about the equipment that you will need to be a writer. Writing for pay today is much more than sitting down at a typewriter and stroking the keys. Today's technology has provided an array of very valuable tools for you, tools that will increase your productivity and save you drudgery. We'll cover the basic tools, progress to the advanced tools, and show what they'll do for you and how to integrate them into your work plan.

Today many people have computers, which make writing and sending out your work easier in many ways. However, a computer requires more knowledge to operate than a typewriter. E-mail and electronic submissions make it possible to shoot your query, article, or book through the wires with the speed of light, and digital photography is close to making conventional film cameras obsolete for many purposes. We've even seen "e-publishing," with several well-known authors producing books to be distributed over the Internet, bypassing paper and printing. These technological advances have eliminated or mitigated many problems that used to pose gut-wrenching dilemmas for writers. Overall, the picture for the beginner is a bit brighter today.

Chapter Eight
What Equipment Do You Really Need?

Many writers start with very little. Although there's a greater array of sophisticated equipment for writers on the market than ever before, you don't need much to begin. It's instructive to remember that many of the great writers in history had no automated equipment, and often nothing more than a pen and ink, or a typewriter.

The reason for hitting hard at this obvious point is that the commercial spirit is deeply rooted, and there are many companies putting out products with strong eye appeal to cater to writers. Anyone who reads the writer's magazines will see the advertisements that support these publications. The ads also indirectly dictate editorial policy. Although some of the products advertised are of limited value, and others are outright useless, the publications will never tell the truth about them for fear of losing advertising dollars. Instead, they'll maintain a discreet silence or publish articles praising the products.

Let's look at a few simple things you might need, and place them in perspective. If you're serious about writing, you'd better get into the habit of treating it like a business from the start, and use sound business methods.

Typewriter

This is essential, despite not having been used by many of the world's best writers in the past. The simple reason a typewriter is indispensable today, if you don't have a computer, is that editors will not read handwritten manuscripts. Let's look at the choices you have, and consider the narrow range of machines suitable for your craft.

You can begin with an office machine or a portable. Your choice depends on whether portability is important. It's now possible to get an office typewriter with a memory, several typefaces, and a spelling checker. Many of the electronic typewriters we see today are really stripped-down word processors.

If you're a war correspondent writing in a foxhole, the manual portable is for you. Otherwise, an office model or a laptop computer is more serviceable. We'll discuss laptop computers later in this section.

Your choice of typeface is between pica and elite type. These terms refer to the type size, rather than to the type style, although there is a typeface known as "pica." Pica type has ten characters to the inch, elite twelve. Because pica letters are bigger, they're easier to read, which is why editors prefer pica type.

Another advantage of pica type is that the word count, important to many writers and editors, is somewhat easier. It's commonly accepted that pica type gives about three hundred words per double-spaced page. Elite type requires some calculation because there are no standard formats.

Price is usually a consideration for the beginning writer. Typewriters are cheaper. A small manual portable, bought at a garage sale, goes for very little today because of technological obsolescence. A top of the line electronic typewriter, with all of the bells and whistles, costs more.

Other Office Equipment

How much do you need, and how elaborate should it be? You may be surprised by how little is essential. Of course, you should have a quiet place to work, but you don't have to have a separate office in your home. A back room, or the back patio will do. Some authors have turned out entire books sitting at a folding table on the back patio in the early daylight hours.

A desk is nice, but not essential. You can keep the essential equipment and accessories in a cardboard box. A work-table, or a folding typewriter table, will do as a start. If you have a computer, you can make your computer desk your workstation. A box of paper and a box of envelopes are all that you really need. Spare typewriter ribbons or spare ink cartridges for your computer's printer are essential.

You may need a camera and other photographic equipment in certain instances. We'll cover these in the appropriate chapter.

Do you need a separate business telephone? Not really, but you might consider another line for your computer if you spend much time on the Internet, as you don't want to miss telephone calls because your line is always busy. It's good to have a telephone for your personal use, and to give the number to editors so that they may contact you quickly if they wish, but don't be surprised if you get very few calls. Usually, editors don't like to receive phone calls, and do not call their authors unless they need to reach them quickly. Today editors tend to use e-mail a lot.

Another point about the telephone, possibly the most important point, is that telephone commitments often mean nothing. Editors often forget what they say on the phone, and if you accept a verbal go-ahead, you'll sometimes find that the editor thought he'd said something entirely different. It's always best to secure any commitment in writing.

You'll also need a telephone answering machine because as a one-man show, you'll be out on interviews and other errands when some important calls come in. You don't want to miss these, and you'll find that calling back promptly will lubricate your relations with editors. When selecting an answering machine, choose a model that allows you to get your messages from a remote location by dialing your number and punching a code. Most of today's models have this feature, and you'll find it helpful, especially if you make many out of town trips.

Caller ID will also be useful, because today many unwanted junk calls come in. Caller ID helps you know who is calling you. Both the answering machine and Caller ID will help you screen out junk calls. Telemarketers typically don't want you to know who they are, and you'll see "OUT OF AREA" or "UNKNOWN CALLER" showing on the Caller ID display when a telemarketer calls. Junk callers never leave a message and you can ignore these. The simple way to avoid wasting time with these pests is to let the answering machine take an unknown caller. A legitimate caller will leave a message for you. You can pick up such a call when you hear the person's voice.

Has your phone ever rung while you were in the bathroom? If so, you'll appreciate a portable phone that you can take with you. Remember, though, that a portable is less secure than a landline, and don't discuss anything you don't want eavesdroppers to know. The 2.4 Gigahertz models are top-line, and are digital, which makes it much harder for a casual eavesdropper to listen in to your calls.

You should also consider whether you need a cellular phone. A cell phone is handy when you must make phone calls while traveling. You might have to call the person scheduled for an interview if you're held up in traffic, for example. You might want to call home and pick up the messages on your answering machine. Whatever your need, be careful when using a cell phone, because there is also a great chance of eavesdropping on your conversations with these as well. When choosing a cell phone, it's preferable to get one that handles both analog and digital modes, because the multi-mode type will work over a wider area.

Remember that anything you say goes out on the air, and might be overheard. Also, don't act like the goon driving a Lexus or Cadillac who keeps one hand on the wheel while holding the cell phone to his ear with the other. Pull over if you have to make a call. No call is so urgent that it's worth risking your life.

Another point is to keep your cell-phone turned off except when you're making a call. Telemarketers are very aggressive, and you don't want a horde of these burning up your expensive airtime while pestering you to buy their wares.

In addition to the basics of paper and envelopes, you will find a few other office supplies useful, but not absolutely necessary. File cards are useful to keep track of your efforts. You should have a card for each manuscript, story idea, or outlet you have, so that you can hold a summary of your entire working information in the palm of your hand for quick scanning and review. This will help you keep track of where you are. Also useful are a stamp pad and address stamp, some stacking trays, and an assortment of pens and pencils. Always remember, though, that these items take up space.

They're not expensive, but too many can get in the way and it can be very annoying to have a permanently cluttered desk. It can also degrade your efficiency.

Good Business

Let's skip lightly over a theme we'll replay at various points in this volume — your writing should pay for itself. Don't spend money on new or trendy equipment unless you really need it. Don't buy anything you can't afford. There are many temptations facing you, and many opportunities to buy the latest, most sophisticated, and expensive equipment, but play it smart. Make your writing pay for itself.

Chapter Nine
The Computer

Years ago, we'd occasionally see a "debate" in a "writer's" magazine between a proponent of computers and a "traditionalist" who maintains that they're unnecessary and do more harm than good. These articles are worth ignoring thoroughly, because they're the result of an editor's trying to generate interest with an artificial controversy. This is a well-known editorial trick, but it can cruelly mislead people who are just starting out in writing.

Let's look at the hard facts about computers:

They're expensive. A computer is more costly than a typewriter. This means that anyone thinking of writing for pay will have to consider carefully whether the investment is worth it. On the other hand, you may already have a computer at home. If not, you may wish to wait until you earn enough by writing to pay for one.

A computer won't make a writer of you. You have to do that on your own. This should be fairly obvious. Much of the world's great writing, and its mediocre writing, too, was done before computers existed. The recent flood of computers, available at prices that many can afford, hasn't made us into a nation of great writers.

Well, if a computer can't do that, what can it do? It can save you a lot of drudgery, that's what. Don't think that all of your working moments will go to creative writing. You still have to send out queries, compose outlines, and address envelopes. This is pure "donkey work," but it still has to be done.

The computer stores information on magnetic disks and prints it out upon command. These are called "files." A file of publishers' addresses saves a lot of looking up and retyping.

You can also have "boilerplate" paragraphs stored for instant recall. You often have to type something like this:

"Please review my submission and let me know if you approve. For your convenience, I am enclosing a self-addressed, stamped envelope. Your timely response is greatly appreciated. Thank you.

Yours truly,

John Smith
123 56th Street
Anytown, USA"

There's no creative writing in this. Although you can't truly classify time spent addressing envelopes as "nonproductive," you can and should seek ways to speed up the process to save your time for the real work. Saving on drudgery can leave you fresh for the work that requires serious thought.

Another problem arises if and when you need another copy of what you sent. It's rare for the postal service to lose a manuscript, but it can happen. If you've kept a carbon, you can retype another original. If you have it stored on a magnetic disk, you don't have to do all of that laborious "keyboarding." You merely have to "print out" another original copy.

This can be a true time-saver in other instances. As we've seen, some editors don't reply to queries. Others may reply, but not return your query. Yet others will return the query with their comments on it. You'll want to try another editor, but you can't send a carbon or photocopy, as this makes a bad impression. Many editors hate to receive "sloppy seconds" and that's what a copy is. With the text of your query stored on a disk, you can print out a fresh copy with just a few keystrokes.

It's aggravating, but some editors will "sit" on a manuscript for months before rejecting it. Some will even start to edit it, penciling in comments and corrections. Others will put a paperclip on it. Yet others will staple the pages together. In certain instances, editors can handle your manuscript very roughly. One editor regularly stapled the photographs to the manuscript. Sooner or later, you'll have the experience of getting a manuscript back and finding it dog-eared, and in generally poor condition. This sort of treatment is evidence of the inconsiderate attitudes of some editors. Some will rub salt in the wound by including phrasing such as this in the accompanying letter: "We wish you luck in submitting this article to another publication." Fat chance, if the manuscript's in bad shape. If you have it on a disk, you can use the returned copy for scrap paper and print out a fresh one. Likewise, if you use a digital camera. Digital picture files are not vulnerable to stapling.

A computer can help you to improve the quality of your writing. Read that sentence again. Read it a third time. The meaning must be crystal clear. A computer cannot improve the quality of your writing by itself. It can't write for you. It can, however, help you to help yourself. Here's how:

If you type a manuscript with a typewriter, you immediately set the words on paper as you type them. You get no chance to review your text before getting a "hard copy." With the computer, it's different. The computer displays it on the screen, where you can sit back and take a look at it before committing yourself to printing it out. If necessary, you can revise it as many times as you need, without wasting paper.

If you make a mistake with a typewriter (even a "correcting" typewriter), and don't catch it immediately, you're faced with a dilemma. Is the mistake important enough to justify tearing the page up and retyping it? Often, if it's not too glaring, you'll let it go. You can't spend your career retyping everything.

With a computer, you don't have to retype a page. You recall the text onto the screen, make your correction, and print it out again. Electronic corrections are great labor-savers, and they eliminate the dilemma of deciding whether to scrap a page for a minor error or letting it go as is.

The amount you'll save on paper and ribbons is small, and won't even come close to paying for the computer equipped with a word processing program. What you'll save in time and frayed nerves, however, makes it all worthwhile. Now let's look at the technical side of computers and how you can use one for word processing, Internet access, and graphics.

The computer can perform several tasks, such as database, spreadsheet, Internet access, in addition to word processing. Computers today are much less expensive than they were years ago, making them affordable for most people starting out in writing.

The heart of the computer is the microprocessor, also called the "chip." This is the miniaturized "brain" of the computer, and is a tiny oblong of metal, plastic, and rare elements about two inches square, at most. The chip controls everything the computer does, when properly programmed. Chips come in different models and speeds. There are economy models, such as the Intel Celeron, which is very adequate for word processing and most Internet access. At the high end, there is the AMD6 and the Pentium III, and faster chips are on the way. These are better for processing graphics, and this is important if you get into digital photography.

The chip or chips (some computers use more than one) are in the "central processing unit," which is the part we normally think of as the "computer." To operate the computer, you also need a keyboard and a monitor. The monitor is a high-resolution cathode ray tube, like a TV screen, that displays your program. It also displays graphics as part of the program. You type in your text using the keyboard. A "mouse" is a device attached to your computer that controls an arrow on your screen, and serves to issue commands to the computer. To print out the manuscript, you need a "printer." All of these devices are lumped under the term "peripherals."

There is one dominant operating system for personal computers, Microsoft Windows. All computers need an operating system to work. The operating system controls the computer's functions, and is designed to accept a variety of "applications programs," such as word processing. A new contender is Linux, which has acquired a following because of its reliability, but which at the time of this writing has fewer programs written for it.

There are also many brands of computers. Some are name brands, such as IBM, Compaq, and Dell. Others are generic "IBM clones," made with foreign components and sometimes referred to as "China 'R Us." Both name brands and the generics are of very high quality. Both come in several different models, some of which are "modular." This means that they can be custom-fitted with several different features. Every central processing unit (CPU) comes with several "bays," slots that accept various types of disk drives. There are usually extra bays provided to allow you to mount whatever types of drives you need.

A basic feature is the "hard disk" drive. This is a sealed unit that fits in one of the bays, and its capacity can be ten "gigabytes" or even more. As a "kilobyte" is a thousand bytes, a "megabyte" is a million bytes. A "gigabyte" is a billion bytes. This huge storage capacity is becoming increasingly necessary because of the huge size of many programs. Normal practice is to store programs on the hard drive, where they're convenient for loading, and files on separate floppy discs.

Computers come with one or more single floppy disk drives. A floppy disk is a magnetic disk that stores the permanent memory. The computer's software, or program, comes on a floppy disk or a CD-ROM, and saving the files requires a disk. Today the standard is the 3.5" hard-cased disk with a 1.4 megabyte capacity. This is barely enough today because many files are very long, and you'll probably need a high-capacity disk drive. One such is a "ZIP" drive, which comes in 100 MB and 250 MB models. However, disks cost between $10 and $12 each, an important point to consider when an editor asks that you send a disk along with your manuscript. If your submission is text alone, a 3.5" floppy disk can hold it, but if you send digital pictures with your manuscript, these will probably take up more capacity than this type of disk can hold.

There's a solid reason for using the hard drive for programs and the floppies for manuscripts and other files. The hard drive may "crash," become temporarily unusable or permanently damaged. Hard drives rarely fail, but when they do the results can be catastrophic. If worse comes to worst and you have to replace your hard drive, you can always reload your programs. If you store your working files (manuscripts) on the hard drive, you'll lose these as well.

If you keep your working files on separate disks, it's extremely unlikely that they'll all fail at once. You may lose your hard drive's contents, but the files on which you've worked so hard will be safe. Any magnetic disk is susceptible to damage, and sometimes this damage makes the information on the disk impossible to recover. Redoing an entire manuscript can be painful, which is why most people who use word processors make "backup" copies as they go along. Backing up means saving your work on a second disk, so that if your primary work disk dies, you'll have a second copy. It's smart to back up your work every day, to minimize the chance of loss. An expedient way is backing up your hard drive.

What's this? Why back up your hard drive, which might crash? No, that's not irrational. The chances of both your working disk and your hard drive crashing at the same moment are infinitesimal.

Your computer is also likely to have a CD-ROM drive because today many programs come on CD-ROMs. Most modern programs are too large to fit on a 1.4 megabyte disk. A CD-ROM disk holds 650 megabytes, enough for most programs today.

An important accessory to have on your computer is a CD-RW (CD-Re-Write) drive, a drive that can write a CD-ROM using a laser. This serves several purposes. First, it allows you to back up your important files periodically. The tremendous capacity of a CD-ROM disk can take probably all of your current manuscripts. It also serves as cold storage for manuscripts you've already sold but want to keep. As we've seen, a CD-ROM can hold up to 650 MB, the capacity of six ZIP disks or over 460 3.5" floppy disks. It's a very compact way to store large amounts of information.

Why would you want to keep a manuscript already sold and in print? If it's a book, you may receive a request for a second edition years later, and it's much easier to begin with the original electronic text than to try to type it all over again. This is where a computer can save you a lot of time. You simply put each chapter on your screen and revise it as necessary, instead of typing it from scratch.

Another purpose of a CD-RW drive is to "burn" a CD to send along with your hard copy, the paper manuscript. As we've seen, magnetic disks are vulnerable to damage, and this can happen with magnetic fields and X-rays. A magnetic disk can arrive at your publisher totally "corrupted," that is, unreadable. A CD-ROM is not vulnerable this way, and can be damaged only by heat that melts the plastic. There's also a slight chance of physical damage, such as under the wheels of a forklift, but this is remote.

CD-ROMs are also much cheaper than ZIP disks, selling for about $40 for a pack of 50 disks. At this writing, they've been on sale for less, and the price is sure to drop further in the future.

Their price is an important reason for sending your manuscripts on CD-ROMs. The low cost makes them expendable. One editor, to whom I'd sent a manuscript and digital pictures on a $12 ZIP disk, told me flatly — "We don't return disks." As a writer depending on his good will, I was in no position to argue. This was the incident that decided me to buy a CD-RW drive.

Another option on the computer is the size of the "RAM," the "Random Access Memory." This is the built-in working memory that the computer has. The absolute minimum for professional use is 64 MBs, because it's necessary to "load" the memory with the word processing program before you can operate the computer as a word processor, and this takes up a lot of space in the memory. You also need spare memory to work with as you write your manuscript. At least 128 MBs is desirable for graphics and for Internet access.

Extra memory is available in plug-in units, and it's possible to upgrade the computer at the time of purchase or afterwards. With the PCs and the clones, it's very easy to do. Other types of personal computers have different capacities, and some cannot accept plug-ins at all.

Another item to consider is a modem. This allows you to send and receive information over your telephone line and is essential for Internet access. Most computers have internal modems, but you can also purchase external modems if your computer does not come equipped with one.

A scanner costs about $100 but can be worth its weight in gold if you receive a request to produce a second edition of a book you wrote a long time ago and do not have the original text on a disk. The scanner allows you to scan the pages and convert them into word processing files, thereby saving you the work of re-typing every word.

Another purpose for the scanner is to copy photographic prints. If you take all of the photographs needed for an article or book with a digital camera, you won't need the scanner, but if you have to use photographs supplied by one of your sources, you may need it if your publisher specifies that only digitals are acceptable.

Buying the Computer

Should you buy it already assembled, or buy components from several different outlets and do it yourself? There are pitfalls in the computer market, and some products and services are designed to catch the unwary. Should you buy it on the Internet, where you often can find rock-bottom prices? There's a lot to say pro and con.

Buying from an Internet source is like buying by mail order. If there's any problem with the computer, and you have to return it for replacement or repair, you must ship it back to the vendor which is both expensive and inconvenient because it deprives you of the computer for a time. The money you save may not be worth it.

Buying the computer system from a local dealer usually means one stop, and writing one check. The dealer also has the responsibility of providing you with a functioning system. With the various types of programs, operating systems, and printers, there is a factor of incompatibility to consider. Many of them are adaptable to various systems, by means of selector switches and "installation" programs. For example, most programs are designed to be adaptable to several different computers, and it's necessary to "install" the program onto the computer before using the program. Likewise, today's printers can be set up to work with many word processing and digital photo programs.

The "install" program presents a number of questions, relating to the type of equipment on which you're using it. You must answer these correctly or the program will not install properly. If you don't know the characteristics of the equipment, you must either find out or have a specialist install the program for you. Don't worry too much about this, though, because today's installation programs are very good and easy to use, much better than they were years ago. Most will scan your system to determine the types of components, and will install your new program automatically.

You can do it yourself, if you read the manuals carefully. They usually give very complete and explicit directions. If you need to hire a specialist, expect to pay him about $75 an hour or more, and the time needed may be as much as two hours.

You may find that buying each component separately allows you to obtain the best price. If you know your way around a computer, this is the best way to go. Keep in mind that you then bear the entire responsibility for making the system work. Each dealer, if you ask him, will tell you that his responsibility extends only to the equipment he sold you, and not to making it work within a possibly incompatible system. This is also the case if you buy your equipment second-hand. You can find some terrific bargains, but it's up to you to make them work with your system.

Unless you're already a computer whiz, you'll want to buy the computer assembled and ready to go. Another reason for doing so is economy. Almost all computer outlets today sell "plug and play" packages, computers ready to go once you turn on the switch. These come with a hard drive, one or more floppy drives, a CD-ROM drive, a modem, a monitor, a mouse, and a printer. They also come with several basic programs already loaded, and these typically include word processing, graphics, and Internet access. There are, however, some points to observe.

What do you really need? The first point is choosing between a desktop and a laptop model. The typical laptop has a built-in keyboard and monitor, a hard drive, one or more disc drives, a modem, and a battery that will keep it going for several hours without recharging. Modern laptops have a "touchpad," a compact device that performs the same function as a mouse. Keep in mind that laptops cost much more than desktops, partly because of the extra cost of miniaturization but mostly because of economy of scale. There are many more desktops manufactured than laptops, and this drives their cost down. Also, a laptop is not quite as compact as many people believe, because you'll still need a printer, and a quality printer is often more bulky than the laptop.

The only justification for a laptop is if you work on the road a lot, and need to write your articles as you go, printing them when you return home. The laptop allows you to work in your hotel room, or even in your car at the side of the road. Some travelers use their laptops on airliners, although they have to observe certain restrictions imposed by airlines because at times laptops can interfere with the plane's electronics.

A major limitation with laptops is battery capacity. They run only a few hours on a charge, and you must plug them into a 110-volt outlet to recharge at intervals. Some have an adapter that plugs into your car's lighter socket.

You also have to decide between the two basic types of computers available today; Macintosh and IBM-type. Macintosh users claim that Macs are better made and easier to operate than IBM types. They are also more expensive, because IBM and IBM clones are far more popular. If you decide on an IBM, as most people do, you'll find economy of scale working for you.

We've noted that today computers are cheaper than ever before. It's possible to buy a basic computer, with monitor and printer, for under $1,000. If you're considering this, after reading some computer outlets' ads, think twice. Then think again. First, these packages typically come with a 15" monitor. For occasional use, a 15" monitor will do, but for someone who uses a computer more than an hour or two a day, a larger monitor is desirable. When deciding on the model you want, consider carefully paying the extra bucks for a 17" or even a 19" monitor for your desktop, because the larger screen is easier to see. If you're buying a laptop, you don't have this choice. You have to accept the monitor built into the model you buy, and these rarely exceed 15". A smaller monitor can work for you if you're using your computer only an hour or two a day, but the small screen can lead to eyestrain if you're working many hours.

It used to be that monochrome monitors were best for word processing because color monitors had very coarse screens, but today's color monitors are very sharp. However, make sure your monitor has a .028" dot pitch or smaller. A monitor with a coarse dot pitch is not as sharp, and this is important when you use it as a tool for work.

Always check a monitor out before buying. Never take the salesperson's word on this point. Always see for yourself. It may be surprising, but some famous brand computers come packaged with fairly poor monitors.

This point is so important that you should dig in your heels and refuse the machine if the monitor doesn't look right to you. Never accept any salesperson's explanation that "you have to get used to it." A bad monitor will cause you eyestrain and perhaps even a headache, and you'll be miserable using it.

Packages also come with a low-end inkjet printer. This may be adequate for printing manuscripts, but won't do for graphics. You might also prefer a laser printer, because the ink won't run if wet. However, a laser printer won't print color photographs, which you might find desirable. A good inkjet printer suitable for printing high quality photographs will cost you $300 or more.

When considering a particular model, also look at the price of ink cartridges. A less expensive model may take cartridges that cost more than those for a top of the line model. Also take a close look at printer speed, and never accept factory claims as truth. Most printer manufacturers will tell you that their printers will turn out a certain number of pages a minute. This is almost always optimistic. In real life, connected to your computer, almost any printer you buy will be slower than factory ratings.

This is especially true when printing color. A manufacturer will tell you that his printer will, for example, print 10 pages per minute in black, and seven per minute in color. This is misrepresentation by omission. The printer will probably work near its rated speed for "spot color," which means a page that's mostly black type but with headlines in color. If you're printing four-color, which is the technical term for color photographs, you'll find that it takes 10 or 15 minutes to print a single page at the highest quality setting.

Another point relates to package deals and rebates. You'll find some packages selling for $600 or $700, with rebates, and when you see this type of offer, always read the fine print. These rebates include signing a contract with an Internet Service Provider (ISP) for several years. Keep in mind that there's nothing free in this world, and that you pay for what you get one way or the other.

The ISP may not be the one you want. As we'll see, ISPs vary a lot in quality of service, and you can judge which you'd like by reading various readers' surveys in computer magazines. These rate ISPs by customer satisfaction, and some rate far better than others. We'll discuss this further in the Internet chapter.

Also, if you already have a computer and are seeking to upgrade, you may also have an Internet Service Provider. You don't need another.

There are many reasons for caution when buying computers and peripherals. The market is laden with booby-traps for the unwary, and you don't want to waste your money on inadequate equipment and unnecessary services, such as a service contract.

Get the best computer you can afford. The reason is that progress is rapid, and if you skimp today, you'll need an upgrade sooner.

The Service Contract

When you buy your computer, the salesperson may also try to sell you a service contract. This is especially true of the mass merchandisers, who make huge profits on service contracts. You may hear a short sales talk on the high cost of spare parts, and how the service contract "protects" you against the cost of unexpected repairs.

This is hogwash. You're better off without one. Here's why.

Electronic components, such as computer chips, need to "burn in" before they're totally reliable. This is done at the factory, or happens during the first few weeks of use by the customer. If they're going to fail, they generally do so within this time. Practically all computers and accessories come with at least 90-day guarantees. If your computer holds up this long, the chances are overwhelming that it's going to last a lifetime. This doesn't mean that you can drop it off the desk, but the fine print in service contracts excludes such accidents from coverage.

There are exceptions. The components vulnerable to wear are the keyboard, the disk drives, and the printer, because they're all electro-mechanical components. Devices with moving parts tend to suffer wear, some more quickly than others. Nevertheless, it's an unusual keyboard or printer that wears out in a year.

Disk drives are unusually rugged and trouble-free. They occasionally need cleaning, but far less often than the manufacturers of cleaning kits claim. Also, when they fail, the cost of replacement is low. Never use a dry disk system to clean them. The dry disk has an abrasive that causes unnecessary wear. The best cleaning kit is one that has a nylon fiber disk and a small bottle of cleaning solution. To use it, you drop about a dozen drops of the cleaner onto the disk, insert it, and let the drive run for about thirty seconds. You should only clean your drive every three months, at most. Most disk drives will work perfectly without cleaning for a year or more.

Another problem with service contracts is that you're locked into the dealer with whom you have the contract. Payment is always in advance. This means that he's got your money, and you've got to wait for his convenience for any needed work. Hard experience has shown that the dealer will assign his repair people to work on the cash customers first, so that he may collect the money. The service contract work can wait. The situation is much the same as with auto dealers, where warranty work takes last place.

This is where you can get hurt. You may be in the middle of a manuscript that must meet a close deadline. If the dealer holds you up, you'll have to swallow your anger and live by his rules.[1]

If you don't have a service contract and the dealer says that he's busy, you can get your machine repaired elsewhere.

The odds are that he'll find a way to accommodate you, because he knows that if he lets you walk away, your money will walk away with you. If worse comes to worst, you can replace a failing component instead of repairing it. Keyboards suited for word processing cost about $20. Printers vary in price, with about two hundred dollars as rock bottom for a letter-quality printer. The money you save on the service contract will pay for several of these components, which you surely won't be replacing every year.

Software Programs

The computer without a program is inert. The program is a set of recorded instructions that tell it what to do and how to do it. The basic program, which comes installed on most computers, is the Microsoft Windows operating system, and you need a mouse to work with it. Windows contains a set of commands that you can activate with your keyboard, as well as "subroutines" that the computer follows without detailed instructions from you.

You then have to consider applications programs. There's a huge variety of programs available at prices from zero to about one thousand dollars. The reason some programs cost nothing is that they're "public domain" programs, and not copyrighted.

Cost and quality don't necessarily go together. The program market is so filled with a variety of goods that it's impossible to generalize. Some programs, costing a fraction of what the very expensive programs cost, are as capable, or very close. In other instances, you may be tempted to buy a program which has many "bells and whistles" on it, but which you don't need enough to justify the inflated price.

You're interested in word processing, so let's concentrate on this type of program. First, don't bother reading any program reviews or evaluations in computer magazines. Get recommendations from friends, or take the program that's bundled with your computer.[2]

How Word Processing Works

A word processor is a program that composes documents that you type. What should a word processing program be able to do? There are certain functions that are essential, and others that are just gingerbread. A lot depends on what sort of writing you do, and the amount of convenience you wish. Let's look at some of the features.

All programs have certain basic features, such as those to open a file, save a file on the disk, and rename, print, copy, and delete a file. They also have lists of different functions and their commands, called "menus," which you have displayed on your screen for convenient reference.

The basic text writing and editing features are also common to all programs. On the screen is a glowing dash, dot, or rectangle called the "cursor." This indicates where the next letter will print or where the next function will take place. There are commands to move the cursor up or down, right or left, one space or to the end of the line or screen. You can also move the cursor to the beginning or end of the file. Your mouse can move the cursor for you. Merely move the arrow to where you want the cursor, and click once on the left key.

It's also possible to "scroll" the screen, which means moving the text up or down, as you wish. This is useful for reviewing a chapter. While so doing, there are commands for deleting a letter, word, or line. It's also possible to insert a new letter, word, or line. If the new material makes a line too long, the program will reform the paragraph, moving excess words to a lower line to keep within the limits. Another command enables "overwriting," which is typing new letters on top of and replacing existing text.

Practically every word processing program, however basic, has an "insert" feature, and this may be the most valuable one of all. At some time in your writing career, you'll surely have come to the end of a manuscript and decided that you should have mentioned something in the middle. You then face a big dilemma. If you decide to insert another paragraph, you have to tear up the pages from that point on and redo them, if you're using a typewriter. With a word processor, you scroll back to where you need to make the insertion, and type it in. The program will automatically move the rest of your manuscript down, and arrange it properly on the pages.

Word processing programs today have very sophisticated insert features, allowing you to put another file at a place you designate in your manuscript. Some, such as Microsoft Word, even allow you to insert a digital photograph where you wish.

As with a typewriter, there are format commands built into word processing programs. Some enable you to set and release tabs and margins. Others set line height, the space between lines. "Word wrap" takes care of words that are too long for the line and which would run off the page. Word wrap automatically moves the entire word to the next line. There's also a function to hyphenate words for a more even right margin. It's also possible to "justify" a page of text. This means having even margins right and left. The usual typewriter format is flush left and ragged right, but with a word processor you can have both margins even. Another command centers text on a page.

There may be special effects available. Some possibilities are boldface type, double-strike, underline, subscript, and superscript.

Other commands center around "block operations," which means moving text within a file or to another file. This is also called "cut and paste." There are commands for moving a line or paragraph. It's also possible to copy a block of text for use elsewhere. There are also find-and-replace functions. A command, followed by the wanted word, will have the word processor find that word wherever it occurs in the text. You can then choose to leave it as is, or replace it. There's also a "global" find-and-replace function, which will automatically seek out every occurrence of a designated word and automatically replace it by another, which you choose when keyboarding the command. You may have a short story with the name "Charlie" in it, and decide you'd rather name this character "Earl." You can have the computer find every "Charlie" and replace it with an "Earl."

All of these features make a huge difference between writing a manuscript in the traditional manner and doing it electronically. It's also important to use good judgment when composing a manuscript, as some features are useless and others are counterproductive.

It always helps to number your pages. The headline feature is worth its weight in gold because editors like to have the article or chapter title and the author's name at the top of every page. They sometimes have accidents, such as dropping a stack of manuscripts off the desk, and reassembling them in correct order is easier if each piece of paper is identified.

Many special effects are useless for manuscripts. Boldface can serve for headings, but an editor will usually choose his own style when he marks up the manuscript for the typesetter. Many editors prefer to see a manuscript with simple word wrap, without any hyphenating and splitting of words. This avoids confusing the typesetter, who may not know if a word's split or hyphenated.

There are other features of modern word processing programs which are excellent time-savers. One is the label feature, which allows you to print a single label or a page of labels from an address on the screen. Some will address an envelope, including your return address in the upper left-hand corner. A truly valuable feature is the automatic word count, which provides a precise figure for the length of your manuscript.

Learning to Use Your Word Processor

How do you learn to use a word processing program? There are courses in word processing offered at various community colleges and business schools, but your best bet is to teach yourself. Why? Because most courses simply take too long. They're designed with the material spaced out for the slowest learners, and if you're bright enough to be a writer you're going to be chafing at the slow pace. Another important point is that there are many word processing programs in use, and the course may be only a general one, and not geared to the program you intend to use. The commands are not fully interchangeable between different programs, and you'll face the annoyance of having to "unlearn" some of what you learned in the course and relearn to suit the program you've bought.

Most word processing programs come with "tutorials," which may be in disk or book form. A tutorial is an operating manual and a set of lessons. Most are well-designed, and are what we call "user-friendly." This means that they're easy to understand, learn, and work.

In practice, you can probably teach yourself how to perform the essential operations in a couple of days. If you need more information, the manual and the lessons are next to your desk for quick reference.

Conversion Programs

There is no single dominant word processing program, and you'll probably find many publishers that use one different from yours. This is why you'll find a program that converts a file from one program to another useful. Some conversion programs will even produce a Mac disk, formatted for use in a MacIntosh computer, and this can be very useful if one or more of your publishers uses a Mac.

Electronic Submissions

Many publishers today want electronic submissions. You can send them a disk instead of a paper manuscript, or send your manuscript electronically, over a telephone line. This requires both the sender and the receiver to use a "modem," which is a device that translates computer language into a form that transmits easily over the phone lines.

A major factor in publishers' asking for electronic submissions is speed. You can save several days' time over "snail mail" by squiring your article and digital pictures over a telephone line. Another reason for sending the article on disk is that it saves the publisher the time and expense of "keyboarding," paying someone to retype your article onto his computer.

Saving Time

The computer saves you a lot of time and aggravation. You can produce a second copy of a manuscript, along with digital photos, in case anything happens to the first one, and it will be as good as the "original." This is critically important if your manuscript gets lost in the mail or on the editor's desk.[3]

This is also extremely valuable if the editor mutilates your manuscript before rejecting it, or keeps it for an unreasonable time without coming to a decision. You simply print out another copy and send it to another outlet.

Summing Up

This chapter hasn't given you instructions on how to operate a computer or word processor. That wasn't the intent. The purpose was to provide you with a rough sketch of what modern electronic wizardry can do for you, and to serve as a guide to choosing one. For those who make the right moves, and good selections, a computer can be a great time-saver. It frees the user from drudgery, and lets him concentrate on creativity.

Notes:

1. Better believe it. This happened to me.
2. One example is my Microsoft Word program. I'd used several others, and my favorite for ten years had been Wordstar. Microsoft Word was harder to use than Wordstar, but I quickly became used to it and made good use of its extra features.

3. One editor recently phoned me to say that he'd lost the file folder containing my article, and needed me to send him the digital pictures right away. I was able to send them to him via e-mail within an hour, getting him out of a jam.

Chapter Ten
The Internet

A major change in technology, the Internet, has affected writers as much as it has the general public. The Internet has already produced major changes in our culture, and we haven't yet seen all of its effects.

Today writers, as well as people in other occupations, use the Internet for both business and pleasure. There are many benefits and pitfalls related to the Internet, and we'll examine these closely. The first step is selecting your Internet Service Provider (ISP).

Selecting Your ISP

In the past, Internet Service Providers offered very primitive services, and charged by the minute. Internet access was a time consuming task because of the primitive tools provided, and the meter was running. Today, many ISPs offer unlimited time for about $20 per month, and there are premium services available in some areas.

Not all ISPs are equal. Reading the consumer satisfaction surveys in computer magazines reveals that there are serious differences in quality and consistency of service. Some are excellent, with quick access and very helpful customer support. Others provide very poor service, and you'll find that you often get busy signals when you try to log on. With some, you'll find yourself arbitrarily disconnected at times.

Another problem relates to advertisements that take up screen space. Before deciding on an ISP, look at the screen you get when you log on to the service. Is it chock-full of ads, leaving only a little space for the material you're seeking? You'll be better off with an ISP that doesn't make its ads too obtrusive.

We can't get into individual ratings here because ISPs vary over time and locale. One that offers poor service today may clean up its act tomorrow. Another reason is that Internet service varies with the area. One ISP offers very good service in California, but is weak in New Mexico.

Before deciding on an ISP, ask your friends for their experiences with various providers. This will be your best guide. Also remember that price alone is not important — what you get for your money is!

The Basics

For Internet access, you need a computer equipped with a "modem." This is a neologism, a contraction of "modulator-demodulator," a term in use 30 years ago. The modem squirts data over your telephone line, which is your basic access route to the Internet.

Unless you live somewhere without postal service, chances are that you've already received many offers from ISPs. These usually include a CD-ROM with the program, and instructions on how to sign up for service. Some computer outlets offer rebates on computers provided that you sign up with an ISP. These deals are usually not worth considering.

The Internet access program consists of an automated "browser," which allows you to log on automatically, and navigate the Internet once you're connected. Browsers allowed the Internet to expand rapidly, making it accessible and convenient for millions of people, because navigating through the Internet used to be a slow and difficult process. The two main competing programs are Microsoft Internet Explorer and Netscape.

Using the Internet

Different people use the Internet for different purposes, from prowling the porno sites to serious research. For the beginner, the starting point is using a "search engine." This is a site on the Internet that allows you to conduct a search for a certain topic or type of site.

Within the Internet is the "World Wide Web," and sites located on it are called "Web Sites." Web sites may be devoted to information on various topics, sites advertising a certain company's products, sites for buying everything from books to motor vehicles, and of course, the ever-popular porn sites.

Some critics have called the Internet "anarchy" because anyone can start his own site and post information on it, valid or not. This is why, when using a search engine, you'll encounter some strange sites, and you can't accept information in them as valid merely because they're on the Web.

Your Internet browser enables you to find sites. Just type in the site's name or topic on the top line and you'll get a list of web sites relating to your topic. Internet browsers such as Netscape also come with "bookmarks" for various popular sites already loaded, and you can click on these to find a list of search engines, among all the other sites. Search engines are tools that allow you to seek out sites that contain the information you need.

Search Engines

Some popular search engines are "Lycos," "Alta Vista," "Google," and "Yahoo." There are also "meta-search engines," such as "Dogpile," which put your search request through several other search engines and display all of the results. You may find these most useful because every individual search engine scans only a small part of the sites on the Web.

There are some tricks of the trade you can use to make your Internet search more effective. A major problem is that a search can turn up a flood of sites, and it will take you a long time to scan each one for the information you're seeking. One way to narrow your search is to use "limiters," additional words to narrow the search to the area you want. For example, if you're seeking information about World War II, you might use the key word "war." However, this will bring you information on many wars and other topics allied to war. Use the precise term "World War II" to focus directly on your topic.

"World War II" might again be too broad, if you're interested in only one aspect of that war. If you're interested in only the diplomatic history of the war, include additional terms, such as "diplomacy." If you're seeking only information on Soviet diplomatic efforts connected with the war, also include "Soviet Union."

The reverse is also true. If your search has turned up no results, you may be using too narrow a focus. Try using a broader term.

Another problem may be that the term is not the same as used by a particular web site. If you're looking for information on "Black Power," it may not be available under that term. You might try "race relations" instead. Likewise if you're looking for information on codes and ciphers and can't find what you need. You might try "cryptography" instead.

Most search engines have advanced features that allow you to refine your search. You can refine your search by including extra key words, but you can narrow the focus by excluding certain terms. Each works slightly differently, but in general you can instruct the search engine to look for "war" but exclude "World War I" and "Punic Wars."

A serious problem with search engines is the electronic trickery that many web sites use to force themselves on you. Some search engines look for key words, and they scan each web site's "metatags," a list of key words contained within the site to make searching quicker. Some web sites purposely include irrelevant key words within their metatags to attract more searchers, because each "hit" means that their advertising banners go on display on the screen. This is in keeping with the aggressive commercial spirit that makes the Internet difficult and time-consuming to use today.

Some web sites are very troublesome to use because they're just "banner farms," with most of the screen space taken up with ads. Others cause problems because they're slow in downloading. The banners always appear first, leaving you staring at the ads while waiting for the material you're seeking. You may want to avoid these.

Bookmarks

One very valuable feature of your browser is the "Bookmark" or "Favorite" function. "Bookmark" is Netscape's term, while Internet Explorer uses "Favorites." Their function is the same. Both allow you to store the URL, or electronic address, of a web site automatically in a list. When you want to return to a particular web site, you bring up the list and click on the name of the site, and the browser takes you there.

Some of the sites you may want on your list are those of news organizations, publishers, and sources of information you can use. If you're writing an analysis of current events, on-line news can be very valuable. If you're writing a piece of fiction that takes place aboard a cruise ship, find a cruise line web site for detailed information about their cruises and ships.

E-Publishing

E-publishing is a brand-new field, and received wide notice when author Stephen King produced *Riding the Bullet*, selling hundreds of thousands of copies. E-publishing makes it possible for the consumer to buy and download the text of a book from the publisher's web site, often at a cost much lower than buying a comparable paper version. The publisher doesn't have to have the book typeset or printed, enabling significant savings that he passes on to the customer.

While it's too early to tell the size of the bite that e-publishing will take out of the traditional paper book market, it's clear that e-publishing has its limitations. You need a computer and Internet access. To read the book, you either have to take your computer with you or print the text, using a printer.

By contrast, it's possible to read a traditional paper book anywhere, even without a computer and no source of electricity. For sheer convenience, nothing beats a traditional printed paper book. This is why the optimists predicting the demise of conventional publishing are premature.

Several e-publishers are:

www.softbook.com

This company publishes Stephen King's *Riding the Bullet.*

www.mightywords.com

www.glassbook.com

www.barnesandnoble.com

Environmentalists may hail e-publishing as a way of avoiding cutting down trees. Certainly, an e-book uses no paper, but trees are renewable resources, unlike fossil fuels, and there's no danger of running out of trees in the foreseeable future.

The Internet: Culture Change

The Internet has brought about a change in our culture. Part of this change is in the way authors work. Today, authors and anyone else who knows how to use the Internet can find information more quickly and conveniently than ever before.

Computer technology has also affected photography, and we'll study how in the next chapter.

Chapter Eleven
Photography for the Writer

Depending on the type of material you write, you may need to provide photographs with your manuscripts. If you can submit competently done photographs, you'll have an edge over the many writers who can't.

Photographs for Publication

Let's start by defining what a "competently done photograph" is. For most applications, it's one whose image is sharp and consists mostly of middle-tones. This means that there should be no large dark areas or any so bright that they're lacking in detail. The printing process has a limited tonal range compared to that of photographic paper. Ink on paper produces a black that is less dense than that of photographic printing paper. The whites are also less bright, because paper made for printing lacks the "optical whiteners" incorporated in good quality photographic paper or photo-quality computer paper.

How sharp is "sharp?" Publishers convert the tones of photographs into small dots of various sizes to simulate shades of brightness and/or color. These are called "halftones." A photographic print or a transparency should have detail at least as fine as the dot size in the halftone. This is a good rule of thumb, but difficult to interpret at times, because it's not always easy to predict the final size of a reproduction on a printed page. When you send in a print or a transparency, you don't know what size the editor will scale it to.

This is a distinction that many photographers and writers fail to understand. Some submit "exhibition quality" prints that are visually superb but don't reproduce well because most of the important detail is murky or burned out. The offset printing process, which is what most publications use today, is better than the zinc plates and rotogravure techniques used in the past, but it's still not ideal for reproducing fine separations in tones or important detail that's too dark.

Let's also eliminate what isn't necessary in photographs for reproduction. We find some myths in photographic magazines, where some ill-informed writers copy each other's work, including the mistakes, and thereby perpetuate these myths.[1]

Let's start by demolishing one common myth.

There are no "professional secrets" in photography or the graphic arts. There are some people who still believe this, and are intimidated by the thought that the "pros" and "old-timers" have a repertoire of "secrets" which guarantee success and which they won't share with newcomers. Anyone with an alert mind and a high school education can learn all he needs to know about photography. There are no "secrets." It's a matter of both book knowledge and practical application, despite the allegations by some veterans that experience is the only way to learn the trade. This is even truer of digital photography, because there are no "old-timers" in this brand-new field.

The "old-time" photographers and editors are dying out, leaving the field clear for modern technicians. This is all to the good, because the old myths are gradually dying with them.

It used to be standard that the print should be 8″ x 10″, and on glossy paper. This came about simply because commercial photographers use this as their most common size, and advertising agencies often used such glossy prints for their work. Because of this, the belief arose that this was the most successful formula.

Photographers in previous years have had to struggle with marginal lenses and films, and one way of ensuring the sharpness of their photographs was to use large negatives. These were often 4″ x 5″ or even larger. A smaller negative was not sharp enough to enlarge, so they would make contact prints. Although some experimenters were producing high quality 35mm photographs in the 1920s, the materials were unreliable, and the processing techniques verged on the exotic. By the 1930s, some news photographers turned to Rolleiflex cameras, with their 2¼″ square format. The 1950s brought a revolution in photography because high-resolution lenses became commonplace, and films improved to match. This was a transitional period, however, and many still thought that only the large format negative could produce a decent print.

We also find a similar myth regarding color photographs. Some believe that nothing less than a 4″ x 5″ transparency will do. Others grudgingly concede that 2¼″ square is an adequately large format. Actually, a sharp 35mm transparency will produce a page size enlargement. 35mm is also very good for black and white work. The image size in modern high-quality digital cameras is much smaller than the 35mm format.

The 35mm format is one of the best for photography, partly because of its versatility and partly because of the high quality obtainable by those who know what they're doing.[2]

Modern lenses and films play major roles in permitting extreme resolution in photographs.

The Camera

Most 35mm cameras are very good, with extremely sharp, computer-designed lenses. Today, the limitation is not in the optics, but the mechanical components, because lenses can resolve more than most films can record.

Generally, the Japanese cameras lead the field. Some good brands are Nikon, Canon, and Olympus, because of their quality of manufacture. When we speak of "quality of manufacture" we are not referring to features. Quality means that the controls operate smoothly. The shutter, when it clicks, does so with a barely audible "whir," not a long, harsh, grating sound. A camera mechanism that vibrates noticeably during the exposure can destroy sharpness and degrade the quality of the photograph.

There are several ways to test your cameras, but nothing beats taking photographs and scanning the results. Following a friend's recommendations also helps, if the friend is knowledgeable.

If you have another format of camera, don't rush to trade it in on a 35mm. It may well do perfectly for what you need. Judge your needs from your experience in producing photographs for pay, and buy only what you need.

One advantage of the 35mm format is that there are many cameras that take interchangeable lenses. This is not as significant as it may seem to some. In practice, the normal 50mm lens is suitable for at least 95% of the photographs needed. A wide-angle or telephoto lens is necessary in some instances. If your subjects are usually groups of people in small rooms, a wide-angle will be useful. Other situations may call for a long lens, if you truly can't move closer to the subject.

Which long lens do you need? An excellent innovation is the telephoto "zoom" lens. It's larger, heavier, and more costly than most other single-focus telephotos, but it's extremely versatile because it can replace a number of lenses in your inventory.

If you read the photo magazines and their test reports, you may read that zoom lenses aren't as sharp as fixed focal length lenses. Technically, this is true, but in practice it doesn't matter. Sharpness is usually measured on an optical test bench, because this is a laboratory technique that assures valid results. On a real camera, using real film, it's much harder to differentiate between them.

Many high-quality lenses can resolve about 300 lines per millimeter on an optical test bench. Most films in common use will not resolve half that, and many are good for only about 75 lines per millimeter. When you consider possible sharpness degradation resulting from camera movement and shutter vibration, the practical limit drops even more. Finally, consider the size of the final product on the printed page. Most printed photographs are smaller than 5" x 7". Because of these factors you can get away with as little as 25 lines per millimeter resolution on the negative.

This is why a variable telephoto (zoom lens) can save you both money and weight. You need to carry only one lens to replace half a dozen others. A good range is the 75-250mm lens. The shortest focal length it provides is 50% longer than the normal lens, which is a useful increment. The maximum provides a 5x enlargement, or telescopic effect.

During the last few years, another film format, Advanced Photo System (APS) came on the scene. APS cameras use film cartridges smaller than 35mm, and the image size is significantly smaller. However, these deliver surprisingly good photographs for their small size, and many have zoom lenses. Their main limitation is that only color print film is available, and it's unlikely that film manufacturers will offer black and white or color transparency films because the format has not been the commercial success they had expected.

Another point relates to automatic cameras that automatically set the exposure and are self-focusing. These have been in development a long time, and the first models were not very good. Today's automatic cameras, in 35mm, APS, and other formats, require only that you point and shoot, and they produce a good picture under most conditions.

Films

There's a bewildering variety of films available, because competing companies are eager to capture what they see as their share of the market. All films fall into one of several rough categories. We'll look at the ones likely to be of concern to you here. Let's look at black and white films first:

- *Slow, high-resolution films*, such as Ilford Pan-F and Kodak Panatomic-X. These sacrifice sensitivity to provide extremely fine grain and extreme sharpness. They often permit an exposure of about 1/50 second at F.11 in daylight. Under good conditions, such films will deliver at least 16" x 20" enlargements and often larger under ideal conditions.
- *Medium-speed films*, such as Kodak Plus-X, with an ISO rating of 125. These films slightly compromise sharpness, yet can allow exposures in a variety of lighting situations, and for this reason are extremely useful. Their sensitivity allows exposures of about 1/250 second at

F.11 in daylight. With correct exposure and development, it's possible to obtain 11″ x 14″ full-frame enlargements consistently. The important aspect of these films is their versatility. They're fast enough to allow exposures in many low-light situations, yet give enough image quality to permit making very good enlargements. Combined with modern cameras, and lenses faster than F.2, they can cope with all but the worst low-light scenes. For most reproduction, the medium-speed films will do. After all, how often do we see a need for an enlargement greater than 8″ x 10″? The standard magazine page is about 8½″ x 11″, and most book pages are smaller than that.

■ *High-speed films*, such as Kodak Tri-X, and Ilford HP-4. These sacrifice sharpness for speed, and the daylight exposure is approximately 1/500 second at F.11. They're almost too fast for normal use. With enhanced low-light performance, these can cope with practically everything except situations that require a super speed film.

Under most situations, Kodak Tri-X will allow an enlargement of about 5″ x 7″, which is enough for almost all newspaper and magazine applications. In reality, very few halftones are larger than this, and most are indeed smaller. Slightly better sharpness, and somewhat better tonality can be produced using the Ilford HP-4. This means that it reproduces fine tones better, and separates close tones.

A new class of films is Kodak "T-Max," in 100 and 400 rated speeds. These are very high-resolution films that will develop in most developers, although Kodak makes a special "T-Max" developer, at a higher price. The 100-speed film is somewhat shy on speed, compared to Plus-X, but it's extremely sharp and can produce almost grainless enlargements.

There are also super-speed films, with speeds up to ISO 3200, for photographs under extremely low light. These sacrifice sharpness and grain for speed, and are useful only when nothing slower will do. We won't consider the super speeds in detail because there's little use for them and they sacrifice everything for quality.

Let's now look at color films. For reproduction, transparencies are best. Some publications will consider color prints, but these are so inconsistent that many will insist upon transparencies. Color prints tend to be bad, despite some fairly good materials available. The reason for the low quality is that they're typically budget prints made by commercial photofinishers working through drugstores. When a color print costs a quarter, you can't guarantee quality.

An excellent film for reproduction is Kodachrome 25, which produces transparencies. Kodachrome's sharpness over the years has built its reputation. Of course, the camera must be good enough to make best use of it. A Kodachrome 35mm transparency can "blow up" to full-page 8½" x 11" easily.

For situations which require somewhat more film speed, Kodachrome 64 is the next choice. This has somewhat more than twice the sensitivity of Kodachrome 25, at a barely perceptible sacrifice in quality. Most editors can't tell them apart.

A recent arrival is Fuji Velvia, about as sharp as Kodachrome 25, but processed in E-6 chemicals, the same that process Ektachrome. For you, the practical advantage is that you can have your transparencies in a day or less, while Kodachrome must go to a special laboratory that can handle it. This can take a week.

In the higher speed brackets, there's a wide choice of films. Any film that delivers good, crisp transparencies will do. Ektachrome has speed, but it's important to understand that there are several different grades of Ektachrome, as there are several different speed grades of foreign films. The higher the speed, the less sharpness you can expect. You'll also see more graininess.

There are some super-speed color print films, such as Fuji 800. You can judge what's possible with these by looking at articles in photo magazines that feature them. These articles are, of course, "rah-rah" articles that bring out the best of these films. These articles also don't mention the shortcomings. The publications go to all lengths to avoid offending advertisers. You can be sure that extremely skilled photographers shot the best photos they could with the films, and discarded anything that was not quite right. What you'll see on the printed page is the best attainable from these films, not what you can expect in everyday use.

Other Photography Equipment

If you're skilled in photography, you may want to do your own processing. It pays to do black and white, because the chemicals and paper don't go stale as quickly as color materials do. Unfortunately, color processing chemicals last about two weeks after you mix them, making color processing uneconomical unless you have many rolls of film to do at one time.

Film processing requires a developing tank, a few bottles to store the chemical solutions, and possibly a changing bag for loading the tank. All of this costs less than fifty dollars, unless you shop at the highest-priced store in town.

Developing black and white is simple, following the manufacturer's instructions. Unless you're very knowledgeable and experienced, follow the developing times and temperatures closely, because the films work best when processed as recommended. It's possible to gain some speed by "pushing" the processing, but overall it's unwise. If you need more speed, use a faster film.

Developing color takes more steps, and requires closer control of temperature. This is for the advanced photographer only, and as mentioned before, is uneconomical unless there's enough volume to support the purchase of a color developing kit.

Making black and white prints is not horribly complex. It requires an enlarger, some developing trays, and enlarging paper. Two good papers for your purpose are Kodak Polycontrast Rapid III RC and Ilford Multigrade. There are several reasons for recommending these papers:

- They're both commonly available. A perfect paper that's obtainable only by special order or from a faraway source is worse than useless.

- Both have latitude, which means that they're easy to use because they forgive mistakes.

- Both are multiple-contrast grade papers. This means that you can change the contrast of the print by using a filter in front of the enlarger's lens. The alternative is to stock several boxes of single contrast grade paper.

- Both are resin-coated papers. Unlike the old types of photographic papers, these don't absorb water readily, and dry very quickly, without special equipment.

- These papers will develop in a processor, or in a tray. They're "stabilization-type" papers, which means that they contain the developing agent within the emulsion.

They don't require a "developer" to bring out the image, but merely an "activator."

- Finally, these papers are controlled mainly by exposure. Leaving them in the developer longer produces little increase in density. This means that if you have to make more than one print you can simply expose and throw them into the developer as you go, without worrying that they'll get too dark.

Processing by stabilization is a technique using a small processor, a device with rollers that drives the paper into a tray of activator, followed by a tray of stabilizer, a chemical which prevents further development. This is a quick but not too dirty technique, and provides a finished print in less than a minute. Drying time is only a couple of minutes more. Keep in mind that a processor can easily cost a couple of hundred dollars or more. You might prefer to use conventional trays. These papers will develop more quickly, requiring less than 30 seconds in the developer. This saves a lot of time in the darkroom.

You'll find an enlarging meter helpful, a real time-saver. If you've been accustomed to exposing test strips before each print, you'll find that a meter will provide the exposure in a few seconds, and is on the money about 95% of the time.

An anti-static brush helps because it's practically impossible to find a completely dust-free room to use as a darkroom. Even if you had one, opening the door to enter would bring in airborne dust. This can be very troublesome if it settles on your negatives, as dust produces obnoxious white spots on the prints. You can remove them by using a fine brush and special dye, called "spotting dye," but prevention is quicker. An anti-static brush contains a radioactive element that ionizes the air around the brush, neutralizing static electricity that makes dust cling to film.

Buying Photographic Equipment

You can find some good buys in the second-hand market. This is especially true when shopping for an enlarger. The new ones are often not as well made as those of a couple of decades ago. Mechanical qualities are as important as optical ones in an enlarger as well as in a camera. Almost all enlarger lenses made during the past two decades are more than adequate for your needs. You can buy a new lens if the one that came with your enlarger is inadequate.

A good idea is to find a photographic dealer whom you trust and to stick with him. This helps to assure satisfaction with what you buy. He's less likely to want to risk losing a regular customer.

The Finished Print

What size prints should you make? There's a simple answer — make what the editor wants.

Most editors don't specify print size, but if they do, it'll be in the guidelines. If they don't, don't ask. Give them 5" x 7" prints. If they object, they can say so. The reason is that some editors will, if asked, say that they want 8" x 10" prints. This is habit, not real need. A 5" x 7" print is more than adequate for most publications. A simple way to tell is to look at the size of the photos on the printed page. There are many photographs much smaller than 5" x 7", and many publications reduce to almost postage stamp size.

You should provide a caption for every photograph, whether black and white or color. A peculiarity of the writing trade is that editors don't like overly long, turgid manuscripts, but they prefer authors to go somewhat overboard on captions. For some reason, they don't mind editing captions to size. If possible, make your captions more than one sentence long, and write a paragraph, if possible.

Always include more photographs than necessary. The reason is that editors often use photographs to fill space on a page, and an excess allows them more latitude and freedom of choice. Editors appreciate this, and will think a little more kindly of writers who understand their needs.

Digitals

Today, we're going through a major change in photography because of computers and digital cameras. The traditional basic principles still apply, but their execution is radically different when you use a digital camera. First, there's no film. Instead, your camera stores the images on a solid-state device. Next, you don't use chemicals or a darkroom to "develop" the pictures. Instead, you load them into your computer and process them electronically. The prints come out of your inkjet printer, in normal room light. From the moment you press the shutter release to the finished print is only a few minutes.

You won't need most of the information in the preceding section if you use a quality digital camera. Let's define that first. The current top-of-the-line digitals produce images with between two and four megapixel resolution. "Pixel" is the contraction for "picture element," a dot that represents a detail in the scene you're photographing. A "megapixel" is a million pixels. Obviously, the more picture elements a camera can record, the sharper the image will be.

Right now, top digitals sell for between $600 and $1,000. This is rapidly changing, and next year they may cost much less for the same specifications. The new top ranking cameras will probably resolve five or six megapixels for about the same price range. What this means to you is that if you have any doubt, or are a little short of money, delay buying a digital. You can be certain that prices will drop soon.

Most digitals run on a set of "AA" batteries, and most record images on a removable "card," a solid-state device that you can insert into a card reader attached to your computer. Card readers cost less than $100, and are worth having because they can upload pictures more rapidly than the connector cables that come with most digital cameras.

There are several types and brands of cards. The "CompactFlash" type is popular, and comes in different capacities. The smallest can hold about 8 MB, and they go up to 160 MBs right now. Larger capacities may be available in the future. A 2 Megapixel image takes up about one megabyte of space on a given card, and the greater the card capacity, the more pictures it can hold. Other brands of cards are the Sony "Memory Stick" and the "Smart Card."

Also newly available is the IBM Microdrive, a subminiature hard drive about the size of a CompactFlash card but slightly thicker. This can hold over 300 MBs and right now is the largest capacity image storage device available. It's important to note that digital photography and technology is a rapidly expanding field, and new devices keep coming. During the next few years, we can expect to see equipment that will make today's best offerings seem pale.

Card type is important, because you probably will need more than the card that comes with your camera. Cameras come with small capacity cards, and if you want to store a hundred or more pictures, you'll have to buy larger capacity cards. You'll end up with several hundreds of dollars in cards, and this may be a problem if you decide to upgrade your camera in a couple of years. Will your new camera accept the cards you already have? If you have an unusual type of card, your choices will be very limited. Before you buy a digital camera, check to see if many brands use the same type of memory card.

The type of image you record will affect the number you can put on a card. Most quality digitals allow you to select the number of megapixels in your picture, and the degree of compression. For professional quality, you want only the maximum megapixels. If you're taking family snapshots, you may be satisfied with lower resolution for the sake of storing the maximum number of pictures, and this will allow you to employ a relatively small card.

The degree of compression affects quality as well. Picture compression is a technique that allows less card space to be used than for an uncompressed picture. Many digitals use the "JPEG" (Joint Photographic Experts Group) system. This system allows several degrees of compression, and this is where you must make a trade-off. You can choose the degree of compression your camera uses. The greatest degree of compression will allow you to store more pictures, at a sacrifice in quality. For professional use, choose the least compression, and buy more cards. Note that some cameras allow storage in TIFF (uncompressed) format, but that these uncompressed images gobble up storage space. As a rough rule, a TIFF image takes up about ten times the memory that a high-quality JPEG does.

The really good news about digitals is the degree of flexibility in use. With a film camera, once you push the button, that picture is permanently on the film. However, you can erase a digital picture from the card, and shoot another. This is very much like using a camcorder, which allows you to record over a tape. This is part of the flexibility inherent in digitals, and you'll find digitals more flexible than film cameras overall.

The bad news is that digitals have certain limitations. The built-in flash is fairly weak, limiting the range at which you can shoot flash pictures. Some digitals will allow you to use an auxiliary flash unit, overcoming this limitation. Another drawback is that digitals have sensitivity equal to only medium speed films, hampering you in low light. Some high-end models allow you to select the sensitivity you want, within a limited range. The maximum at this time seems to be equivalent to ISO 400. Yet another limitation is that you can produce only prints, not transparencies, with your color inkjet printer. At this moment, there is no satisfactory transparency material on the market.

Some top digitals, such as the Nikon Model 950, allow you to shoot both color and black and white pictures on the same card. Black and white format provides somewhat increased resolution.

The real flexibility of digitals over film cameras comes when you upload the images into your computer. There are several photo processing programs on the market, and two widely used programs are Kodak Picture Easy and Adobe Photoshop. These allow electronic manipulation of the images. They will enhance the images automatically, adjusting the exposure to produce a good print. If you have to make further adjustments, they allow adjustment of contrast and color balance, and you can make your pictures lighter or darker, as you wish.

They also print pictures. You can adjust the image size, printing full-page or printing several on a sheet of paper. There are choices of printing materials as well, depending on the quality you need. You can print out a proof copy on cheap copying paper to save time and money, or you can print a top quality print on photo grade paper.

For top quality color prints, you need a top quality inkjet printer. A laser printer will allow only black and white prints. One good photo-quality inkjet printer, as of this writing, is the Epson Stylus 900. Several companies have introduced advanced models designed for high-quality color printing. Some are the Epson Stylus 2000P and the Olympus P-400. These use new inks that resist fading better than the current crop.

Let's note here that, for submitting photographs for publication, a printer is not as important as the quality of digital images you can submit on a disc. The reason is that photo quality degrades with each step, and a publisher will prefer to receive a digital image instead of a print made from that digital image, because with a print, it's necessary to scan it and convert it back to digital format, losing quality each step. A good print is useful as a "proof," to show the publisher a good copy of what is on the disk.

Digital pictures are very versatile. With some word processing programs, such as Microsoft Word, you can insert the photo at the appropriate place within the manuscript, making life easier for your editor. You can also send the digital images as attachments to e-mails, if you editor wants the material in a hurry.

Some editors will ask that you send the pictures in "TIFF" format. This is an uncompressed format that takes about ten times the disc space that JPEG does. You'll find that sending TIFFs via e-mail takes a very long time. If your editor is not in a rush, send your TIFFs on disk. For this, you'll have to use a CD-ROM. Zip disks are too expensive and 1.4 MB floppy disks do not have the storage capacity.

Photographs Can Make or Break a Manuscript

If you can provide photographs with your manuscripts when required, you have an advantage over competitors who can't. You can also earn more money per manuscript, because if an editor has to pay a photographer to shoot some pictures to flesh out an article or book, it leaves less money for the author. Some editors will use "stock photographs," provided by a photo agency. These also cost, and sometimes cost top dollar.

Learning to do your own photographs saves you money. It's equally important that you can also shoot the photographs exactly as you want them, instead of relying on someone else's interpretation. This is why the skill will pay off in both the short run and the long run.

Notes:

1. Where do I get my information, and how do I know that I'm right? Good question. Before I started writing full-time, I was employed in the printing trades as a "cameraman." I had to turn photographs into "halftones" for reproduction. This is how I know what makes a good photograph for reproduction. I've also worked as a photographer at various times in my life. This skill has served me well, because my photographs have served to illustrate many articles and books.
2. It occasionally happens that someone who's not very skilled at photography will view one of my black and white prints and ask me if I used some sort of super film for the negative. I reply that the sharpness is the result of ordinary careful work, not any unusual material or technique.

Part III:
Managing Your Career

Now that you've got a handle on the basics, you're ready to understand the fine points of writing for pay. What do you do when an editor rejects your manuscript? How do you measure how well you're doing? What are the ramifications of using pen names? Will an agent be useful in your career? What about manuscript revisions? Are they necessary or worthwhile? We'll study these and other topics in this section.

Chapter Twelve
Administration

When you begin your career, you'll quickly find that you'll be spending part of your time in non-productive work that is directly related to your business. This is administrative overhead, and you can't avoid it.

As a freelance writer, you're a small business operator, just as if you were operating a gas station or a convenience store. You'll have to handle the routine tasks of administering your business, and the only exception will be that you won't have any employees.

You will have to keep books, entering your income and business-related expenses, which are essential for tax purposes. For this, you may choose to use one of the computerized bookkeeping programs, or you may do it manually. The "Globe" brand of record book is a good choice if you want to do it manually, because it's a simple system entirely adequate for the small business operator. It also offers convenience, because you may not want to fire up your computer just to enter the month's income or expenses.

Be aware that you can deduct many expenses, such as business mileage, but this requires that you keep a daily log of business miles traveled. Keep a small notebook in your car, and record the date and purpose of each trip, along with the miles traveled. You may choose to keep a complete record of auto expenses, and deduct the proportion that applies to your business. However, it's easier and simpler to take the Internal Revenue Service's mileage allowance, which is over 30 cents per mile as of this writing.

You'll have to save your receipts to substantiate your deductions. Let's take a quick look at some of the expenses you'll be able to take out of your taxes:

- *Home office expenses.* This means that you can deduct the fraction of your home expenses that apply to your office, such as rent, mortgage, repairs, utilities, etc. The common way of doing this is to calculate the square footage of your office in relation to the total area of your home. If your office takes up ¼ of the total area, you take off one quarter of your home expenses. One important point is that your home office must be devoted exclusively for business. You cannot deduct a quarter of your bedroom or kitchen.
- *Office equipment and supplies.* This means your computer, printer, ink cartridges, paper, envelopes, and other office items.
- *Business telephone expenses.* This is typically ½ or ¾ of your total bill. Likewise for Internet access, as this is often a part of the writer's resources.
- *Business lunches.* If you take someone to lunch during an interview, this is deductible, according to the IRS.
- *Business travel.* Likewise for travel expenses, if you have to make a journey to cover a story. If it's an overnight journey, meals and lodging are also deductible.

Remember you must save any receipts. Always keep in mind that deductions are not "free money." The government doesn't reimburse you for your deductions. You merely take the deductions off your taxable income, and if you're in the 30 percent tax bracket, all you really "save" is 30 percent.

Other Tasks

Other administrative tasks are ordering supplies, balancing your checkbook, sending out queries, answering correspondence, keeping track of the books and articles you're writing, and filing the paperwork connected with your business. This can easily take up ¼ of your time.

You'll also find that you're the shipping department, responsible for packaging and mailing queries and articles to publishers. You'll also be your own telephone receptionist, and you'll find your writing day interrupted by both important telephone calls and junk calls. You'll also initiate many telephone calls to sources to set up interviews. You'll spend time on the Internet researching information for your articles and books.

It's important not to get behind on administrative tasks. You don't want to wait until your printer is out of ink before buying another cartridge. Likewise for postage stamps, paper, and other expendables you'll need. You'll also have to keep your bookkeeping up to date, because if you throw all of your receipts into a shoebox, you'll have an administrative nightmare at the end of the year. Instead, keep envelopes for the various categories of expenses, and file your receipts accordingly when you do your periodic bookkeeping.

How often should you bring your records up to date? A convenient interval is monthly. It will take only an hour or two to do your end of the month bookkeeping, and you'll find this enough to keep you well organized. Good administration is at the heart of any business, and it will be crucial to yours.

Chapter Thirteen
Tricks of the Trade

Professional writers learn some tricks of the trade from experience. This chapter will lay out a few for you.

Maintaining Confidence

It's easy to lose confidence when you begin writing, or at certain points along your career. Alternatively, there are career milestones that build your confidence. Let's list some that happen to many writers:

You finish your first article or story. It may or may not sell, but at least you know you can carry a writing project through to completion.

You score a hit with a query for the first time. Again, this doesn't guarantee that your piece will see print, but at least an editor has given you a vote of confidence, however tentative.

Your first piece sees print. This is one of the big moments, because it's the first publicly visible sign of your success.

You receive your first check. Seeing your article in print is believing, but actually receiving a check for it is more impressive. It also helps pay the bills.

Your income from writing exceeds your other income. If you've begun part-time, while holding on to your regular job, this will cause you to consider if you should now make the break and write full-time.

You write something on assignment for an editor. If all of your writing assignments so far have been the results of your queries, an editor who takes the initiative shows you that you're in demand.

You sell a previously rejected article or book to another publisher. This builds your faith in your own ability and judgment, because it shows clearly that a particular editor is not the last word.

You're asked to teach at a writing seminar or workshop. This shows that other writers look up to you as an authority, and value your opinions.

Fleshing Out a Manuscript

An article, book, or piece of fiction can be summarized on a single page. In fact, this is what you do when you send a query to a publisher. Once you get the green light, you have to fill blank pages in a meaningful manner. Obviously, you have to insert many details, but at times you might find yourself with a short article or book. There are some ways to add more to your works.

You can add to your manuscript by inserting dialogue, if you're writing fiction, or use quotes if you're writing non-fiction.

Use photographs, if appropriate. This technique is applicable mainly in non-fiction. Many editors feel that photographs make a manuscript more attractive than one that depends on text alone. In fact, many editors will insist that photographs accompany an article, to increase visual appeal.

List sources and references in an appendix. This is especially important in an article for a professional publication, but much less important if you're writing a breezy article for a mass publication. An appendix can contain a list of similar books and articles, and be titled "For Further Reading."

Insert more details. If appropriate you can turn a case history or a case study into a chapter. If you're writing a book on airline management, for example, you can devote an entire chapter to describing how a particular airline handled a series of problems, or built up its routes. Likewise, a book on organized crime can have one or more chapters devoted to particular organizations.

Don't overdo any of these techniques because an editor might think that you're "padding" your manuscript. That can work against you.

Chapter Fourteen
Language Errors to Avoid

We often see abuses and misuses of the language, and some of these errors take hold and become fashionable. They come about not only through ignorance of basic grammar, but because of torturing of the language by people trying to be clever. We can't cover them all, but we can scrutinize a few intensively, as a guide to what to avoid.

Let's first note one important point: we're not going to go by the "King's English." The English used among the educated classes in the British Isles is a form all its own, and unlike English spoken anywhere else, even as close as Whitechapel or Stepney. Hardly anyone speaks what has come to be known as "Oxbridge," and we won't try to base our appraisal of proper English on it. Instead, we're concerned with American English, and a good guide to what's proper in "Americanese" is the Random House Dictionary. We'll also see that many examples of bad language use are not grammatical faults, but errors of style. Let's examine such an example first.

At This Point In Time...

This is a classic redundancy, and anyone who listened to the speeches of former President Nixon will recognize this phrase. Nixon's speechwriter was too clever by half, and he tended to lace his speeches with such gems. Why is this a "redundancy?" Easy. You can replace the entire five-word phrase with one three-letter word: "now."

Government speechwriters are notorious for this deficiency. It may seem surprising that such excellent talent would display such weakness, but there are some contributing causes. First, the people for whom they work aren't very proficient in their native language, and don't recognize the goofs. Therefore, they can't exercise effective supervision, nor correct errors. We also have to understand that these people get "top dollar" for their work. This tends to inflate the ego, and induce a feeling that they can do no wrong.

Finally, the masses tend to expect high-flown phrases from politicians. One who speaks simply doesn't make as good an impression. Flowery phrases are a must. This is why we see redundancies such as "young juveniles." There are no old juveniles. To be a juvenile is to be young, according to the dictionary. However, why use one word when you can make two fit into the sentence? An unnecessary modifier before the noun always helps.

Another redundancy has become a cliché in our language — "viable alternative." It's not enough to use a four-syllable word. Some people need to puff it up with another, unnecessary word.

Yet another redundancy is "serious" tacked onto "crisis." Can a crisis be anything but serious?

The same for the adjectives "qualified" and "competent." We often read something of this sort: "If your car shows symptoms of wheel shimmy, take it to a qualified mechanic." Why anyone would want to take a car to an unqualified mechanic is hard to understand.

Still another redundancy is to tack on unnecessary words AFTER the main one. This produces phrases such as "thunderstorm activity" about which we hear so much from TV weathermen. Also beware tacking the word "situation" onto another one. That can lead to phrases such as "crisis situation" and "negotiating situation."

Big words impress people. It's easy to puff yourself up with five-dollar words. That's why we see longer words used where shorter ones have traditionally sufficed. Doctors use them constantly for that purpose. "Medication" means exactly the same as "medicine," but it seems to have replaced the shorter word completely in American usage.

"Impact" is both a verb and a noun. It means "hit," or "affect." However, it's become fashionable to use the word "impact" when "hit" or "affect" would do as well, because it sounds more impressive.

Adjectives and Adverbs

"...the slow falling snow..."

This phrase was written by someone who used to teach English, and published in a magazine. What's wrong with it? "Slow" is an adjective. An adjective is a word that modifies a noun. However, in this case, it's modifying the word "falling," which is a verb. Any word that modifies a verb is an adverb. Also, any word that modifies another adjective is an adverb. The adverbial form would be "slowly."

This is a basic point of grammar, and one you can pick up in any high school English course or textbook. However, many Americans, including professional writers, never pick up on this. They often simply jam adjectives together without thinking that when there are two or more adjectives that apply to a particular situation, one or more must become adverbs.

There's another way to do this, which few employ. If you want to use another adjective, separate the two words by a hyphen. We can lay out the same example again and say that "...the slow-falling snow..." would be correct.

Corrupting Words

"Optimize," and "normalize" are real words, according to the Random House Dictionary. These are adaptations of nouns, turning them into verbs. However, we won't find the word "prioritize" in the Random House Dictionary. It's not a legitimate word. We do, however, find other examples of erroneously using a noun as a verb.

Another corruption of the language comes about because of a fundamental misunderstanding of a word's definition. This catches on and becomes fashionable. One horrible example is "chemistry," which has been misused to denote the substances used to process photographic film. The correct word is "chemical," or when there's more than one, "chemicals." "Chemistry" is a science and a subject we learn in school.

"Alternative" is a word we often find abused and misused. We often see it used in place of "choice." There's a strict meaning to "alternative." It means one of two choices. If there are more than two choices, they remain simply "choices," although some prefer to dress up their writing or speech with the classier word "options."

Another word often misused is "convince." Some people can't distinguish between "convince" and "persuade." "Convince" has to do with a state of mind. You can "convince" a person of a certain opinion, or fact. "Persuade" has to do with a course of action. You can "persuade" someone to do something.[1] Yet we read or hear of someone trying to "convince" another to do it his way.

Another word misused by many people who should know better is "media." This word is the plural of "medium." A newspaper is a medium of communication or propaganda. A radio or TV station is the same. We can refer to all newspapers, books, and magazines as the "printed media." We can lump printed and electronic means of communication together and call them all "the media." However, to call a single TV station "a media" or "this media" is wrong, however many times you hear it said, see it written, and no matter which trendy people use it this way.[2]

Clichés

Try to avoid current and trendy clichés used as euphemisms. One popular one is "issue." This word is often used as a substitute for "problem," "failure," "defect," or other words that have negative connotations. You may, for example, see this in a press release by your local power company. Discussing a recent power outage, the press release may say: "The issue was resolved at six o'clock on the evening of the 24th."

Another cliché that has come into common use in recent years is "fighter jet." These aircraft used to be called "jet fighters," with the modifier before the noun, but journalistic trendiness has brought about the current form.

Another abused word is "gender," used as a substitute for "sex." A person is one sex or the other. A word may be masculine or feminine, according to "gender." Examples are "his" or "hers," masculine or feminine pronouns. Don't confuse the two, as in "She was not hired because of her gender."

Keep in mind that what's sharp and trendy today can become archaic tomorrow. Lacing your manuscript with trendy
clichés can lead a perceptive editor to the conclusion that
you think in clichés, and are devoid of original thought.

Watch Your Language and Usage!

You can easily understand why it's better to use words
correctly than not. However, making a goof is never fatal to
your career. Usually, it doesn't even cause a ripple. Most
people, including editors, will never spot it.

Notes:

1. *Strictly Speaking,* Edwin Newman, (New York, Warner
   Books, 1974) p. 47.
2. *It Didn't Start With Watergate,* Victor Lasky, (New
   York, Dial Press, 1977), p. 69. Mr. Lasky refers to "a
   media" and its attitude towards President Kennedy. In the
   next paragraph, Lasky uses the word correctly, as a plural.

Chapter Fifteen
Revising Your Work

The question of whether to revise your manuscript and how much to revise it remains murky, and unfortunately the many opinions expressed on this subject often don't clarify anything. This is one question to which there can be only one correct answer, despite the assurances of some "experts" that there can be many.

Revision means going over a manuscript to correct typos, spelling errors, grammatical errors, errors of style and syntax, and to clarify ideas. It can also encompass paraphrasing to condense ideas that can be expressed more concisely.

There have been many books written dealing with the subject of revision. Some encourage a nit-picking "line by line" or "word by word" approach to revision.[1] This takes the author beyond the point of diminishing returns. It's simply uneconomical to write a manuscript and then to do it over several times, which is what this degree of revision entails.

The most important point regarding revision is to strive to do it right the first time. There'll always be a need to go over a manuscript lightly, to correct errors, but anything more than this is worthless. If you've written something that's so faulty that it truly needs such extensive revision, you're better off scrapping it and starting fresh.

A significant exception can be with a well-paid fiction writer. If his work is so much in demand that he can demand advances from a publisher even before starting to write the next novel, he can afford to make many revisions. His work is an art form, and extensive "polishing" and "manicuring" makes it more salable. These are the people who write articles telling how they often tear up five pages at a time and start over, etc. They can afford to do so, if they earn fifty or a hundred dollars an hour.

What does this mean to you? The central point is that you must be honest with yourself. If your skill is not at a level that permits writing something correctly the first time, you can't think of becoming a commercial author. This is a harsh judgment, but it's realistic. There's a bright side, though, which makes it all worthwhile. You'll find your skill and speed improving as you go. It would be an exaggeration to say that an author merely writes the same sentence over and over again, but realistically, there are only about 20,000 words in common use, and putting them together is a task that an author learns. You become more proficient as you go. Your percentage of errors drops consistently. This is what eventually makes your work economical to produce.

Keep a running mental estimate of what your work costs to produce and what fee you can expect for it. You may find that some of your work costs you fifty hours and brings in only a hundred dollars. You earn two dollars an hour. Is this economical for you? This sort of estimating will lead you to the "bottom line" on earning a living with your writing.

You'll find that, as your hourly rate increases, it becomes both more profitable and more necessary to take some time to polish your work. The competition is stiffer with the better-paying outlets, and you need to turn out the very best you can. By keeping an eye on the hourly rate you're earning, you'll know how cost-effective your revisions are.

Notes:

1. This does sell books, though, but mainly to novices and amateurs. They lack the experience to understand that writing must be cost-effective to be profitable, and that earning a living at it entails doing it right the first time, most of the time.

Chapter Sixteen
Problems With Editors

Editors are people who are more ordinary than they'd like to admit. There are talented ones, mediocre ones, and poor ones. They cover the entire range.

The way some editors work will cause their writers problems. Sometimes, this is unintentional. In other instances, it's calculated and a result of the editor's disdainful and disrespectful attitude toward his writers. This results from the excess of writers in relation to the demand. Not only is the competition fierce, but editors tend to undervalue writers, and to treat them as if they were totally disposable. Many editors have the attitude that if one writer leaves, there are several others lined up waiting to take his place. The result is that they cause certain problems for their writers, taking advantage of a writers' weak position and reluctance to complain.

Let's look at some of these problem situations and examine how to correct them. More importantly, let's check out the ways to avoid them.

Editors Who Impose Short Deadlines

Occasionally, an editor will need a piece quickly, to fill a space or because it's timely. This can lead to his requiring you to turn it out to meet a close deadline. Usually, editors don't ask for the impossible. If there's enough time to meet an editor's need, it's wise to try to accommodate him and build up a reserve of good will.

A few editors, however, chronically seem short of time, and request a short deadline for every piece. Unless the publication is a news magazine, this is a symptom of their disorganized style of working. Occasionally, you'll come across an editor who rushes you, but then sits on the piece for weeks or months. You may find it annoying to deal with an editor who constantly cries "wolf."

You may occasionally get a letter from an editor that reads, in part: "Please notify me at once if you can't meet the required deadline. If so, I will have to make other arrangements." If you're a new author, this skittishness may be understandable. He will see you as an unknown quantity, and need the reassurance that you'll meet his needs. A few editors, however, have personality problems and express them this way. We'll examine some more examples of personality problems next.

Editors Who Are Sarcastic

Some editors seem to write with pens dipped in acid, never missing the opportunity to be demeaning to an author. A rejection letter can be polite, less than polite, or have a positively nasty tone. Sooner or later you'll get one of these, and it's best to develop a thick skin and take it in stride.

It may offend you to have to deal with such a personality, but be thankful that you only have to read an occasional letter from them. Other and less fortunate people work with them every day.

The Editor Who Can't Say "No"

The normal process is to send a query, wait for the okay, and proceed with the book or article. The author who follows this without thinking several steps ahead risks getting hurt. It's important for the new writer to pace himself very carefully, and follow the needs of his market. The editor who can't say "no" is the flip side of the coin of the one who is hypercritical and difficult to please.

Some editors over order because they use poor judgment in giving "okays." Others simply don't keep track of the queries they approve and end up with a tremendous backlog of manuscripts, more than they can publish within a reasonable time.

In many instances, they'll be reluctant to take the initiative and admit to the writer that they made a mistake. If you're the writer involved, you'll find yourself happily turning out manuscripts for an editor who seems to be pleased with almost everything you do. After many months, you'll notice that your material isn't getting into print as quickly as you're turning it out, and that the backlog of unpublished manuscripts is growing.

Editors also follow another practice that they carefully avoid revealing to their writers. They overbook, as do the airlines. They don't know how big each issue is going to be. The number of advertisements varies month to month, affecting the number of pages in each issue. They give the go-ahead to their writers for more stories than they can use. This inevitably means that articles sit in file drawers getting old, bypassed by others that editors prefer. Editors are very ruthless in this way, because at all costs they don't want to ever get caught short and not have enough material to fill their pages. This is one of the dirty little secrets of the publishing business. Get used to it.

This is a problem you can avoid. Don't make the mistake of saturating an outlet with your material, no matter how tempting. It's easy to become excessively encouraged when you see your work in every issue of a magazine. It's also very easy to go too far when an editor sends you a lot of assignments.

Measure your market carefully, and note how quickly your submissions are getting published. Always keep in mind that your articles may be getting stale while they're sitting in a drawer. The events about which you write may become out of date if the manuscript sits for too long. How long is "too long?" This depends on the nature of your material. Fiction is generally not as time linked as is nonfiction, and you can estimate if what you write is in danger of going stale. If the editor rejects it later, you'll have trouble selling it elsewhere. As a very rough rule, a year's delay is cause for concern.

Some editors can be cruel when returning an article that has become out of date. They'll include a sentence in their cover letter that says: "Please feel free to submit this article elsewhere."

This is the point when you have to pause for reflection. You need to consider several factors to estimate whether you're vulnerable to being hurt.

First, ask yourself if you're being paid on acceptance or on publication. If on acceptance, you're doing well. You're earning income and what the editor does with your work after he pays you is less important than if you're waiting for payment.

If you get paid on publication, watch out! Even if you have a guarantee that all of your work will be published, you're tying up your property for a long time. You might be able to submit it elsewhere for quicker publication. The more material you have with a single editor, the longer you must wait to be paid.

Another problem can arise if you have unwisely sent him a glut of material, more than he can use. This is a problem of your causing, a problem that forces the editor to choose among your manuscripts. He'll choose the manuscripts he likes best and return the others. It's bad enough that you have to compete with other writers, but competing with yourself is a loser.

You must also consider whether the material is salable to any other outlet. Some outlets are so specialized that you won't be able to give away any material they reject. In this connection, it's important to know how many outlets there are in the field, and whether the material you write is suitable for more than one.

An example is if you write book reviews for a specialized field; let's say hypothetically, bird feeding. How many publishers are there in this field? How many of them seek a book reviewer for books dealing with bird feeding? If your editor rejects a number of your reviews, where else can you sell them?

Sending too much material to one publisher also risks altering the power relationship and causing a further weakening of your position. As an author, you're already in a weak position from the start. Editors and publishers can pick and choose, and many writers fall by the wayside. Under normal conditions, a writer who has talent, and can sell his material to many outlets, can choose to go where he receives the best treatment. An author who has too much material tied up with one publisher takes the same risk a bank takes in making a very large loan.

Normally, if a problem arises, the bank risks only the value of the small loan. However, a multi-million or multi-billion dollar loan puts the borrower in a very powerful position. If he defaults, the bank will be seriously hurt. This is what we've seen with American banks that made loans to third-world countries. The same power relationship applies if a business allows a big customer to build up too much credit. Failure to pay can put the company out of business. It doesn't matter that a lawsuit can recover the money in a year. Without cash flow now, the business goes under.

Apart from putting all of your eggs in one basket, you almost invite the editor to hurt you when you invest too much time and effort in one market.

Double Ordering

Some editors will give the same assignment to two writers. When the manuscripts are in, they'll pick the one they like for publication and return the other. This pits one writer against the other and is unfair because it inevitably leaves one writer out in the cold. It's especially unfair if the editor doesn't tell the writers the game he's playing. Only the most desperate writer would knowingly accept such an assignment, unless he were paid in advance, win or lose. Editors don't normally do this, but it's wise to be aware of the possibility.

Lateness in Responding to Queries

Some editors are very slow in responding to queries. In some instances, they're so slow as to sabotage the article. One editor, for example, received a query about a "First Responder" medical aid course. The writer thought it might make a good article. He asked the editor to give him a quick reply because the course was starting in three weeks. When he received no reply, he assumed that the editor wasn't interested. Two days after the last day of the course, the editor's assistant telephoned the writer to say that they were interested in the article. This was three months after the original query.

Whose fault was it, really? Granted, the editor dropped the ball, and in fact was very inconsiderate about it, but the writer should have been more active in pursuing the matter. He did learn a lesson from this, however, and when the same situation came up two years later, he queried two publications at once, assuming that one would reject the idea and the other would pick it up. He was right, and he got his assignment in time, before the start of the course.

Editors Who Don't Reply to Queries

Some editors will not reply to queries from anyone who does not write regularly for them. Some have enough writers, and won't take the time to do anything but throw a newcomer's letter into the trashcan. This happens whether or not there's a self-addressed, stamped envelope enclosed.

If this happens to you, there's little you can do. You might assume that the post office lost one letter, but not two or three. Although you may be reluctant to give up hope altogether, there's little point in wasting time with such an editor. It's best to move on to someone else, who might be more receptive.

Keep an eye on the publication, though. The editor may change his policy a year or more down the road. Also watch for a staff change. A new editor might be more willing to reply to you.

Lack of Communication

One well-known writer was surprised to find his column dropped from a monthly publication. The editor had replaced it with a column by another author, but had not informed this writer of the impending change.

This lack of communication is discourtesy at best. It can also be a symptom of something more severe. If the editor has decided to discontinue a certain writer, he may feel that the writer is now beneath notice, and not worth the time to send him a note of explanation. This is a reflection of "ego tripping," but there's nothing the writer can do about it.

A greater danger comes if the writer has several articles backlogged with the publication when the change takes place. The articles may or may not have been published, but if they have, the writer may have a hard time collecting for them. The editor or publisher may feel that, as they're not going to use the writer anymore, they have no need of him and consequently no need to keep him happy. They, therefore, stall payment and hope that the writer will become discouraged and give up attempting to collect.

If there are several unpublished articles, the editor may not bother to return them. Unless the author has sent them all via certified mail, he can't even prove that the editor ever received them.

Editors Who Steal Ideas

Intellectual theft is commonplace and hard to prove. Some in the literary world will claim that it never happens, but this is obviously untrue. What's not so obvious is that an editor will sometimes seem to be stealing an idea, because of the viewpoint of the author.

If you query an editor regarding a projected article, you may get a refusal, only to see an article on the same theme appearing a few issues further on. This may seem like blatant theft to you, but it may not be.

Ideas rarely occur to only one person. Another author may have already proposed, or even written, such an article or book. The editor may not tell you "No, thank you, we already have something like that in the works."

Another idea of yours may result in the editor's deciding that, although the idea has merit, you're not the best person to write on it. He then may hand the assignment to another who seems more qualified.

There's little you can do except avoid someone who steals your ideas. An accusation is very difficult to prove. There are very few blatant examples of theft, and even these are sometimes difficult to pin down.

Editors and Publishers Who Advertise

No editor or publisher should have to advertise. Writing is such a crowded field that editors usually have no problem in finding people to write for them. They get all the queries they need, and don't have to seek more. Any editor who has to advertise for writers must have done something to alienate those who have written for him. If you see a magazine advertising for writers, watch out! This is one of the few unequivocal signs of trouble.

The trouble may take many forms. An editor may simply be very hard to please. The publication may have a poor record in paying. If you're tempted to reply to an advertisement of this sort, it's wise to go slowly and be very cautious.

Another type of publisher that usually advertises for writers is the subsidy publisher. This type, also known as the "vanity press," seeks people who are so anxious to see their work in print that they'll pay money "up front."

Another cautionary point deals with "agents" who advertise. The good ones don't have to, because they're in demand. Those who do are either spurious "readers" or thoroughly bad agents. We'll discuss subsidy publishers and literary agents in later chapters.

The Slow Payer

When payment is delayed, it's not usually because of anything the editor's done. Slow payments are the result of decisions by the publisher or comptroller, and the editor is usually opposed because he needs to keep his authors happy to keep the material flowing in. It's best to test the water with one or two pieces and await payment before sending any more.

Slow payment may be one reason for a publication's need to advertise for writers, and this is a possibility to keep in mind when replying to such an ad.

Staff Changes

Time brings changes. Some can be beneficial, and others harmful. You'll find it irksome when an editor with whom you've had a good relationship leaves. His replacement may not be as receptive or helpful.

The other side of the coin is that if an editor with whom you have a good working relationship goes elsewhere, he may take you with him. He may wish to bring some of his writers to the new publisher, and this provides you with a new market.

It may also be that a certain editor has been steadfast in refusing your work. A change of editorship can provide you with a new beginning. This is why it's good practice to keep an eye on any publication for which you wish to write. If the subject interests you greatly, it's worth taking a subscription. You can keep track of format and contents, as well as the comings and goings of the editorial staff.

Remedies and Countermeasures

There are few. The main point is to be aware of the possibilities and take precautions against getting hurt, rather than devising ways to fight editors who pose problems. In some instances, legal action may be possible and even advisable, as in the case of collecting payments that are large enough to justify an attorney's fee.

Keeping your efforts diversified by submitting to as many different publishers helps avoid having all of your eggs in one basket. This minimizes the extent of any particular problem. Fundamentally, avoidance is the best defense.

Chapter Seventeen
Handling Rejections

Rejection slips are occupational hazards for writers. They come in various forms, and are sometimes surprising in content. Some are in boilerplate language, designed to be uninformative. These are typically couched in weaseling words:

> *"We regret to inform you that your submission, though excellent, doesn't meet our editorial requirements at this time."*

The purpose is to save the writer's face by being nonspecific about the reasons for rejection. Editors don't want to start arguments or have running gunfights with writers. They don't have the time.

Sometimes, a rejection letter can seem downright stupid. Here's an example:

> *"At this time, we have decided against publishing the article. You are welcome to submit it to other magazines."*

The wording implies that, because they've decided against publishing the article "at this time," they may consider it in the future. Nevertheless, they're rejecting it here and now.

Why, then, pretend to give you permission to submit it to another magazine? Editors get themselves crossed up, too.

Some editors try to save time by sending out printed forms with a checklist, checking off the appropriate sentences and paragraphs. Such a checklist type rejection notice can look like this:

❑ *We are currently overstocked with this type of material.*

❑ *The material is not within our usual editorial policies.*

❑ *We have recently used similar material.*

❑ *We already have material like this scheduled.*

❑ *The material does not meet our quality standards.*

❑ *Topic is too tangential.*

❑ *Topic is too narrow.*

❑ *Topic is too general.*

❑ *Not original enough.*

Some of the "reasons" listed are not very informative, which is why few editors use this sort of rejection notice. It's too specific for a brush-off, and not specific enough for a tailored rejection.

Many editors take the time to compose each rejection individually. This has its advantages, especially when the author's a regular contributor. Many editors do value their regular authors and want to keep them in their "stable."

Some editors send photocopied rejection slips. This summary treatment can appear insulting to you, but you shouldn't worry unduly. While these are not as common as they used to be, they're still efficient ways of disposing of a nasty problem.

Except for those with personality problems, editors don't like to reject queries and articles. Those who used to be authors know that these have a negative effect on any relationship with an author, and that any author who gets too many from one editor will go elsewhere. An author, in turn, should see the problems of handling rejections from the editor's viewpoint, and understand the pressures of the editor's situation.

There are many possible reasons for rejecting a manuscript. Let's run over some relating to the manuscript or the author.

Poor Quality

The manuscript or query may be ineptly written, because not everyone who fancies himself an author has the skill. Editors are plagued with amateurish efforts every day of the week. Replying to these people only provokes resentment if the editor is honest. Therefore, this person's likely to get a boilerplate letter that says something like this:

> *"Thank you for your recent submission to XXX Publications. We appreciate your thinking of us.*
> *"While excellent in its own right, your manuscript does not fit our editorial needs at this time. We are returning it to you with our thanks, and hope that you will think of XXX Publishers again in the future."*

This letter is pure bullshit. It's designed to save the feelings of the person whose manuscript didn't make it. It's heavy on compliments, delivering "strokes" to soothe the battered ego. Although this letter seems personally written it's probably pure boilerplate taken off a word processor's disk.

Wrong Subject

This, again, is the author's fault. Some writers and would-be writers don't have the good sense to tailor their material to the market. Sending a pro-abortion article to a conservative religious magazine is likely to be a loser. Likewise if you send an article advocating gun control to the National Rifle Association's publications. The reply to this sort of effort is likely to be a similar form letter, or even a photocopy, especially if the editor feels offended by the article.

Not Following Instructions

Some writers simply don't follow the editor's instructions or the writer's guidelines. If the desired format is a manuscript of 3000 words, a writer who submits 10,000 will receive a rejection. Some editors and publishers insist on photographs to accompany the text, and will not take kindly to text alone.

Editorial guidelines are not the whole story, though. The manuscript may depart from what's customary for that publisher. If there's a preference for extensive use of quotes, or heavy characterization, any submission should have them.

Scheduling

An editor may reject a query or manuscript for several reasons relating to scheduling. There may be a similar article by another writer in the works. A similar piece of fiction may have appeared the previous month. The editor may feel that he's devoted too much time and space to this topic, and may be seeking variety. He may, by higher order, be limited to a certain number of articles of one type per year.

Another type of scheduling consideration is the seasonal article. A Christmas theme should reach an editor several months before Christmas, not two weeks before or two weeks after.

Other Reasons

As we've seen, the rejection letter often won't tell you why the editor really rejected it, even when it's a personal letter. Other reasons may affect the editor's decision.

Often, it's simply that the editor has to choose among many manuscripts, and doesn't have a truly sound reason for rejecting one over the other. The editor doesn't want to tell you that, though. Nor does he want to tell you of the casual method of selection. He probably handed several manuscripts to someone else in the office and said, "Here, Charley, read these and tell me which one you like best."

Few editors are absolutely honest and direct enough to admit as one did: "I don't know exactly why, but it just didn't hit me right."

Sometimes it's simply that: personal preference, without any overriding rational basis.

Advertisers and Their Influence

One very important, and little discussed, reason for rejection is the fear of offending advertisers. Some periodical publishers are very sensitive to the needs and likes of their advertisers, and will scan everything considered for inclusion with this viewpoint. If you submit, for example, a "car test" article that is critical of that make or model, it probably won't see print because the publisher doesn't want to lose the big advertising bucks. This characteristic is common to many types of product-oriented publications. Gun, photography, motion picture, motor magazines, and others all seem to follow the same policy: "Everything's wonderful."

This commercial consideration also gives us a clue regarding why there's so much criticism of government in print. The government doesn't advertise the way corporations do. It's therefore always "open season" on government.

Favorites

Editors have their "stable" of writers, but some go a step beyond. Editors play favorites too, which should not be surprising to anyone familiar with the publishing field. In giving preference to their friends, editors may feel compelled to furnish reasons for turning down others' work.

There are many excuses that will fit. The editor can mention characterization, plotting, references cited, syntax, quotes and dialogue, and many other factors.[1] Often, these have little relation to the manuscript, especially as many editors don't read the entire manuscript thoroughly enough to formulate such profound judgments.

Another reason for not taking the expressed reasons seriously is that if the editor truly wanted to publish the article or book, he would reply, "We'll publish your submission if you make the following changes...."

Dealing with Rejections

Don't take rejection slips too seriously. After getting several, you'll begin to notice some odd discrepancies. Different editors will reject the same manuscript for totally different reasons. This is, in fact, a valid diagnostic test to determine whether the problem is with you or it's them. Always seek a "second opinion." A bad manuscript should appear bad to any professional editor, and for the same reasons. If one editor rejects it for characterization, and the next rejects it for plot, try a third. It pays to get a third opinion. A rule of thumb is that when three editors shoot down a query or manuscript, you should rethink the theme. Perhaps it is a bad idea. Perhaps the time is not ripe. Possibly the "slant" is not as good as it might be.

Another possibility resulting from sending a query or manuscript to several editors is that one might accept it. This is the big hurdle to the beginning writer who may be overawed by editors. It's a good feeling, restoring self-confidence and providing incentive to try a little harder next time.

Whatever you do, don't argue with the editor or send him a nasty letter, because this will compromise your chances of dealing with him again. It's also unprofessional. Arguing with an editor is a lost cause.

Recovering from Rejection

A significant milestone in building up your self-confidence is when you send a manuscript rejected by one editor to another who accepts it. This will show you beyond all doubt that your writing is worthwhile, and that you do not have to accept a rejection as final. You'll also feel a lot better about yourself.

Salvaging a Manuscript

You should never treat a rejection as final. It's often possible to salvage a manuscript or at least some components. One way is to resubmit the manuscript in a few months, with a change of title. Surprisingly, this often works. Editors rarely remember all of the manuscripts they read.[2]

If the manuscript is fiction, it provides an opportunity for a word processor to revise it quickly. The search-and-replace function facilitates changing all of the names quickly. This is superficial, but it helps.

On a higher level, a word processor allows shuffling sentences and paragraphs, for a more extensive revision. This can work for both fiction and non-fiction, as it's possible to generate several articles and stories by writing different introductory paragraphs and changing the order of the subsequent ones.

A failed or rejected manuscript need not be a total loss. It can make a chapter in a future book. It's also possible to break apart a book that didn't make it and sell individual chapters as articles or short stories. The professional writer has to be versatile and adaptable. He must not only learn to take rejections in stride, but to make the best of bad situations. Coping by salvaging creatively is an elegant solution.

Rejections are not disasters. They may batter the ego, which is one vital reason why a writer either starts with or quickly develops a thick skin. The true professional does not take rejections too seriously, but learns what he can from them.

Notes:

1. A few years ago, I conducted an experiment. I was acquainted with the editor of a science fiction magazine, whom I knew held strongly left-wing views. I submitted several short stories, each with a strong right-wing theme. One futuristic story dealt with capital punishment, and another presented a favorable view of vigilantes of the future. All were rejected with comments about plot structure, characterization, etc. I reworked the stories according to the reasons given, but still kept the right-wing orientation, and returned them to the editor for future consideration. Not one ever appeared in print.

2. It's only happened to me once in over two decades that an editor returned a manuscript with the comment; "I've seen this one before."

Chapter Eighteen
Understanding Contracts

If you write articles or books, you may have to consider signing contracts. Articles don't always involve contracts, while books almost always do.

A contract for an article is usually simple and straightforward. It will state the title of the article, amount of payment, kill fee, if any, the rights sold, and an affidavit that the seller is the actual author. The contract is usually a one-page affair, and not complicated to understand or interpret.

Book Contracts

Book contracts are very different. They usually involve much larger sums, and a commitment to pay the author royalties for the selling life of the book. They also specify a set of conditions that may or may not be to your liking. Let's take a close look at the hows and whys, because these can be very deep waters.

The Small Publisher

The small publisher usually offers a contract that is stripped down to the bare bones. The contract covers royalty rates, advance on royalties, if any, an affidavit that the seller is truly the author, a statement that he indemnifies the publisher against liability for libel or plagiarism, a listing of the rights sold, and a number of "housekeeping" paragraphs stipulating the way in which the contract shall involve the author's heirs, if any, and the laws of the state under which it is drawn. The usual practice is to sign the contract after the author submits the manuscript. In that sense, the contract is a formality.

The Large Publisher

This is an entirely different situation. While the small publisher offers a contract after the book's written, when he's had a chance to review it and decide that he wants to publish it, the large publisher starts out with a contract. You'll find the large publisher handing you a contract before you begin work on the book. The purpose of the contract is to lock you in to that publisher, just in case you're thinking of seeking a more lucrative offer elsewhere.

The preliminaries may be long and annoying. The small publisher usually gives you a "yes" or "no" after seeing your proposal, or sometimes on the basis of a letter or phone call. The large publisher will usually ask you for a detailed outline, and even stipulate the form that the outline should take. When you send in your outline, don't hold your breath. It then goes before an "editorial committee" or "editorial board." In the tried and true manner of bureaucrats, the publisher's employees cover themselves by splitting the responsibility, so that the blame for a failure can never be laid on only one person.

The major publisher has an organization with clearly delineated functions. Along with the editorial board there's usually a contract negotiator to deal with the author. There's a legal department to draw up the language of the contracts and to review proposed changes. This adds up to a cumbersome procedure. Drawing up a contract with one of these is never simple, and it's wise to understand what to expect, because you'll be dealing on unequal terms.

At some point, you might consider hiring an agent. The agent understands the business and can look out for your interests very well because of his familiarity with publishers, the process of negotiating contracts, and the tricks of the trade. It's harder to "bullshit" an agent than it is an author, especially a new or inexperienced author. In addition, many experienced and successful authors don't have the talent, patience, or emotional stamina to work through the process of negotiating a contract on favorable terms, and prefer to delegate this task to an agent.

Negotiation

The first step is to understand that you'll never be allowed to deal on equal terms. This is so basic that it should be obvious, but many fail to take the point. The publisher's negotiator deals with you, the "principal," directly, but you don't get the same privilege. You won't be dealing with the president of the company. You'll always be dealing with a flunky, although the title will never be exactly that. The person with whom you deal may have a title such as "New Acquisitions Editor," "Contract Editor," "Negotiator," or just plain "Editor." Whatever the fancy title, the person is simply a wrangler. It's his or her job to deal with authors and to negotiate the best possible terms for the company.

This has two distinct and very important implications for you:

1. *You're dealing with a professional, an experienced negotiator who presumably knows all the tricks, while you're a relative amateur.* The wrangler concludes perhaps a hundred contracts per year, while you may negotiate only one or two. The negotiator also knows what the "going rates" are in the marketplace. You may not. Very importantly, the wrangler gets paid on salary, whether or not your particular contract goes through. The contract, therefore, is more important to you than it is to the wrangler.

2. *The wrangler is paid just to negotiate.* You don't get paid for the time you spend. This puts you at another disadvantage because you may become more quickly tired of protracted discussions. You also may not be able to afford so much unproductive time. This then becomes a strong incentive for you to conclude negotiations by agreeing to less favorable terms than you might have had. The ability to hold out for a better offer can be very important.

You'll find that the wrangler for a large publisher will have an arrogant attitude that comes through despite efforts to hide it. You may get repeated reminders that "this is the largest publishing house in the state (nation or world, take your pick)." If you're fairly secure in your own personality, you'll withstand these efforts to intimidate you, and you'll retain more poise during the negotiations.

This adds up to a weak position for you, and you must be very aware of your limitations and needs before starting on these negotiations. You must be aware that you can't "win" in conventional terms. The best you can do is to get an approximately fair deal.

The Rules

There are some unwritten rules. Although they're not set down on paper, they're nonetheless real, and if you ignore them you'll weaken your position. Observe them, even if you don't like them.

The first rule is that the negotiator can impose a delay on the discussions by avoiding responsibility. If you ask for a concession, and he doesn't want to give it to you, he doesn't have to say "no" right away. He can "cop out" by telling you that he must ask his boss, or ask the editorial committee, or refer the matter to the legal department, etc.

You're not totally helpless in this situation. If there's something in a contract that you don't like, you can always say, "I'll have to think about that for a while." The main point is to stand up and demand what you want, without cringing, no matter how intense are the efforts to overwhelm you may be.

Number two is that the first contract he offers you is always a "throwaway," and if you accept it unchanged, you're giving up advantages you might have otherwise gained. The first contract is composed of "boilerplate" and thrown together. It may contain provisions that don't apply to your situation.

Another rule is that you should always ask for more than you expect to get. You can back down more easily than you can escalate.

You may, however, decide to escalate anyway. Don't be afraid to ask for something that you forgot during the first go round. The wrangler is used to this.

Finally, don't take anything the wrangler says at face value. Just because you're negotiating in good faith doesn't mean that he is. If you have reason to doubt the truth of his or her statement, you can quickly resolve the question by asking: "Are you willing to put that in writing?"

The Written Contract

When you see a major publisher's contract for the first time, you may be taken aback by the number of pages and the wide range of topics it covers. This isn't by accident. The publisher employs a legal department to formulate contracts that stack the odds in the publisher's favor. The contract, with all its clauses and provisions, limits the author's rights and choices as much as possible while giving the publisher the maximum possible freedom and discretion.

Today, most contracts are written in plain language because the cumbersome "legalese" formerly used to baffle laymen has gone out of style. In any event, the current tactic is to try to lull people and catch them unaware, not to confuse them.

The contract will describe the work to be done. The book's title may be indicated, and the contract may stipulate the number of words, photographs, and other characteristics of the work. There may be a specification regarding the number of copies of the manuscript that the author submits, and the format that the publisher requires. The contract will usually specify a date by which the author promises to deliver the work.

Some contracts call for the author to compile a table of contents and an index, and to correct proofs. The author may correct typographic errors, and make changes in the text. However, contracts generally limit the amount of text the author may change, except to correct printer's errors. There may be a percentage of alterations allowed, and any excess charged to the author.

Somewhere in the paragraphs describing the work will be a phrase something like this one: *"...in final form and content acceptable to the publisher, in its sole discretion...."* This is a license to kill. It means that after you've finished the book, the publisher can declare your work unacceptable, for any reason, and you have no recourse. While you're locked in to that publisher, he keeps an escape hatch open for himself.

There is a legitimate reason for this "killer" clause. Publishers often contract with new writers, and hate to commit themselves to buy a manuscript sight unseen. Another reason is that even established authors can go downhill, and "burn out."

Some negotiators will tell you that this is standard practice in the industry. Unless you know of a contract without this clause, you can't contradict them. If you've previously had a contract, with that publisher or another, that did not include that clause, you are in a much stronger position. Without that, you have to accept it or decline to sign the contract. If you're bluffing, you may zap yourself out of a writing assignment that you really want. There are, however, ways to "finesse" this. One way is by the expense account, which we'll deal with later.

The contract will assign the rights to the publisher. The publisher generally has the right to copyright the work, produce it in whichever form he desires, sell it where he wishes, have it translated, sell the reprint, abridgment, and film rights, and gain the author's cooperation in advertising the work.

The publisher agrees to publish it at his expense, and to pay the author a certain percentage of the income as royalty. The royalty is usually calculated on net proceeds, not list price, because the publisher wholesales the work to distributors and dealers. Normally, the publisher calculates the royalties every six months, and pays them a couple of months after the cut-off date. This varies from one publisher to another.

The author also stipulates that his work is not plagiarized and is not libelous. He agrees to pay the costs of legal defense against such lawsuits. The author also agrees to obtain written consent if he uses any material from copyrighted works.

The publisher retains certain rights, such as to edit the manuscript as he sees fit, and to be the final determiner of its acceptability. He also may have it printed in the style and binder he chooses, advertise and sell it where he wishes at the price he sets, and have it translated, if necessary.

The contract usually allows the author a small number of free copies, but the author gets no royalties on these.

Some contracts, especially those dealing with texts and other non-fiction, call for periodic revisions by the author. This is a point to watch. Such a clause can tie the author to the publisher for longer than he wishes, and for the same percentage. An author may find that his work is selling extremely well, and may feel that he's entitled to a bigger share of the "take," but the long-range provisions in a contract will close out this option for him.

A clause that provides the "muscle" in such a contract is that the publisher can charge the costs of revisions to the author's royalties if the author is dead, incapacitated, or unwilling to produce them. Often, the paragraph contains the wording "acceptable to the publisher," which is basically a clause that gives the publisher dictatorial powers. The publisher may insist on unreasonable measures for the revisions, or it may be simply an "escape clause." If any contract you see contains this sort of wording, be very careful.

Another contract provision will deal with the division of income from radio, television, or screen sales. There may be a sentence dealing with foreign sales.

The publisher also has the right to decide when sales of the book are low enough to justify discontinuing publication. There's usually a clause dealing with the disposition of the printing plates and residual stock. The author usually can buy these at a nominal cost.

Most contracts contain a paragraph stating that the author agrees not to write or have published anything that may conflict with or harm the sales of the work. This can be a significant booby trap if you're already writing for other outlets. If you agree, you'll be depriving yourself of your present income on the promise of royalties from a book that is still in the future. The only thing to do is to dig in your heels and tell the wrangler outright that you can't agree to any such limitation.

You may incur expenses in writing your book. It's prudent to ask the publisher to cover such expenses. The wrangler's first comeback will be to offer you an advance on your royalties. You should refuse this, because if the publisher doesn't accept the book, you'll be obliged to reimburse him. The reimbursement of royalties is usually a standard clause in a contract anyway, and you should watch for it. Advances are another potential pitfall, because it imposes a financial burden on you if you don't do what the publisher wants.

Another aspect of having the publisher pay expenses is that it's both a test of his sincerity and an incentive for him to keep on with the project. The more you can induce him to sink his money irretrievably into the project, the more you increase your chances of acceptance upon completion. If you can get a written commitment of at least one thousand dollars to cover your expenses, start spending it, and send in the receipts to collect it. Failure to reimburse expenses can be an early warning that something's not right, which is why you should start spending the expense money on legitimate expenses as soon as possible.

Every contract drawn up by a lawyer will contain the standard disclaimer:

> *"This agreement represents the complete understandings of the parties involved and may not be changed unless the parties agree to it in writing."*

Read this carefully, and believe it. This is why you must be very careful if the wrangler tells you something that is not in accordance with the terms of the contract, or tries to suggest that the contract doesn't quite mean what it says. In some instances, a wrangler will tell you to pooh-pooh a clause in the contract. Not so. If you believe that, you'll let yourself in for a lot of grief. Never forget that, although the law states that a verbal contract is as binding as a written one, proving it in court is something else.

If there's any clause you don't understand in a contract, ask for an explanation. If you don't understand that, don't just say "yes" and pretend to. That's very unwise, and the canny wrangler will quickly take advantage of some people's reluctance to admit that they don't understand something.

Contracts are legal obligations. Read and understand any contract carefully before signing, because signing it can have far-reaching consequences.

Chapter Nineteen
How to Assess Your Progress

Writing is a highly competitive business. This is normal for an overcrowded field. Screen and TV actors also find themselves in a similar and intensely competitive milieu. The net result is that for every winner, there are several losers.

You'll surely be concerned with how well you're doing, both absolutely and in comparison with other writers. Gauging yourself is very helpful because it gives you an idea of your standing and also indicates possible areas for improvement.

One way to tell how well you're doing is to compare your income from writing with your needs. The first stage is breaking even. Are you at least covering your costs of paper, film, ribbons and postage with the income from your writing? Are you earning enough of a surplus to pay for new equipment, such as a camera or word processor?

The next stage is trying to earn a living with your writing. How large a part of your living expenses does your writing cover? Can you yet earn a living at it? Are you earning more this year than last year?

A very important point to watch is your exposure. Are you getting into more markets? If not, you run the risk of stagnating, a very real danger. Another way of gauging yourself is comparing how much exposure you're getting compared to your peers. Are you getting as much of your material into print as are others?

It's easy to become complacent. All it takes is a comfortable level of income and regular publication.

When a piece of yours appears in print, do you compare your manuscript with the published version? This can provide some very important information for you. The editor may have revised your wording somewhat, and if he's good, you can pick up some writing tips from this. You may see how he was able to condense a turgid sentence, stating the facts more economically. This is where you can learn some of the fine points of writing.

It's helpful to distinguish between genuine improvement and change for change's sake. Some editors cannot leave well enough alone, and won't let an article pass their desks without revision of some sort. This makes it important for you to ask yourself, whenever you see that the editor's changed your wording, "Was this change really necessary?" You'll have reached a turning point when you find that the editor introduces more grammatical errors and errors of usage than you had in your manuscript. One editor, for example, saw a sentence that read, "A brothel serves as a *nodal* point for other criminal activity," and changed it to "A brothel serves as a *nodule* point for other criminal activity." Unfortunately, the editor was incorrect. "Nodule" is a medical term for a cyst-like growth, and is a noun. "Nodal" is the correct adjective to use, as originally written.

How many typos (typographical errors) did you have in your manuscript? Do you proofread your material before sending it off? Do you check it against the printed version when published? One turning point in your career is when the printed version contains more typos than your manuscript. This may seem improbable to the beginning author, but typesetters and proofreaders are human, too, and they do make their share of mistakes.

Another turning point in your career comes when you get a regular column in a publication, instead of only irregular articles or stories. If and when you're asked to be a magazine's book review editor, for example, it will mean that you've developed some stature in your field. You may be offered a chance to write about a topic that isn't your favorite, but if there's any chance at all, take it. These opportunities are few and far between.

Keep an eye on your performance. You can be sure that others are doing it. Monitoring yourself is a good way to improve your skills.

Chapter Twenty
The Pen Name: Why and How

There's an aura of illegitimacy surrounding the use of a pen name. The clandestine aspect suggests something illicit to conceal. Actually, there are several very good reasons for using pen names, and some famous authors have used them for years.

E. Howard Hunt wrote a couple of dozen spy novels while working for the Central Intelligence Agency. He used pen names because he did not wish to advertise his connection with the C.I.A. at the time. John Le Carre is the pen name of a former employee of the British Foreign Office who wished to conceal his affiliation while still in their employ.

You're probably not an employee of either, but you might have a reason for using a pen name nevertheless. Let's look at some reasons why authors have used them in the past.

One author sought to write an article for a magazine whose editor had had a severe personal conflict with the author's regular publisher. The editor advised the author to let him publish his article under a pen name because he felt that the other publisher would hold it against the author if his work appeared in the pages of that magazine.

In another instance, an author was writing regularly for a magazine whose editor had an ego problem. This editor declared categorically that any author who wrote for another publication would never write for him again. The only logical choice was to use a pen name for a while, until the editor was replaced.

Another author published a number of books under a pen name because of their controversial nature. He did not want to have to take the flak that they might arouse, especially because he occupied a sensitive position. "James Wilson" is not my true name. Why am I using a pen name? For the best of reasons: self-protection. I have some uncomplimentary things to say about some editors and publishers in these pages. If I used real names, I'd get some people angry at me, people whose good will I still depend upon to earn a living. I would not be able to be quite as honest and direct if I used real names, and this would diminish the value of this book.

One of this country's most noted porno stars also writes children's books, according to rumor. True or not, this is an excellent reason for using a pen name in those circumstances.

Yet another regularly published author of nonfiction dealt with topics that might embarrass some of his sources of information if he published under his real name. As a well-known person in his field, he felt that it would be easy for others to reason out which of his contacts had passed the controversial information to him. Because a prime concern of journalists is protecting their sources, this author felt that the best protection would be to use a pen name and avoid laying suspicion on his associates.

In another instance, an author noticed that the contract with his publisher contained a provision that prohibited him from writing for any other publisher. A friend advised him that this is illegal, because it's restraint of trade. However, this author felt that discretion is the better part of valor, and chose not to confront his publisher directly. He wrote for others under a sobriquet, thereby avoiding any unpleasantness.

A very common reason for using a pen name is to suit the material. A female who writes "hard-boiled" detective stories, for example, might find it a handicap if she wrote under her real name such as "Tillie Truelove." She or her publisher might choose to print the stories under the name of "Biff McCoy," "Studs Jackson," or the like. We also find the same name situation with western novels. Two-fisted stories generally have authors with a monosyllabic first name and two syllables in the surname. This is also true of many two-fisted screen actors. Females just "don't go" in this context. One appearing under the name of "Millicent Margate" might suffer in sales because of it.

It can also work the other way. "Millicent Margate" is a splendid name for use with romance novels and confession stories. The real author might be a man named Jeff Luger, a name totally unsuited to the genre.

Finally, we must look at those unfortunate enough to have strange or comical names such as "Lipschitz," "Quackenbush," and "Castleberry." Some authors never publish under their given names for this reason, regardless of genre or outlet.

The beginning author, eager to build up his list of credits, may be reluctant to use an alias. Experience has shown that this isn't a serious concern. After all, it's the money that truly counts, and a list of published pieces is still only a list. If the author's talented and prolific, a few missing pieces won't matter. Alternately, he can frankly admit the use of a pen name when presenting his list to a prospective publisher.

Some of the greatest figures in literary history have used pen names for legitimate reasons. If there's a need, don't hesitate to do so.

Chapter Twenty One
Writing Fiction

There are basically two types of fiction: "mainstream" and "genre." "Mainstream" is the type usually done by the most well known authors, whose novels make the best seller lists. Mainstream short stories also appear in the big national publications that publish fiction. Mainstream pieces may deal with many types of subjects. Some of the most talented mainstream authors are E.L. Doctorow, Evan Hunter, and Sidney Sheldon.

"Genre" is a French word meaning "type," and it refers to fiction restricted to one subject. Some of these types are: westerns, spy fiction, detective stories, science fiction, supernatural, and horror. Stephen King is an outstanding supernatural genre writer. The champion of western writers is the late Louis L'Amour, who died in 1988. He was so successful that any new printing of his novels is certain to be a best seller.

Some literary snobs like to look down upon genre writers as being a lesser breed than mainstream writers. This is nonsense. Some of the genre writers are exceptionally talented in their own rights.

One superb example is the late Isaac Asimov, a sci-fi writer who was also a scientist. Another is John Feegel, a mystery writer who is a forensic pathologist. As we see, successful novelists are not all professional writers. Lucian

Truscott IV is a professional army officer. Joseph Wambaugh was a police officer when he began writing. Arthur Conan Doyle, who created Sherlock Holmes, was a medical doctor. Ernest K. Gann was an airline pilot.

What makes good fiction? Nobody knows for sure. There are many theories regarding fiction, and even more dealing with how to construct plots. Perhaps these have their places, but there's truly only one valid criterion: "Does it sell?"

One important fact to recognize is that a fiction writer is an artist with words instead of paint or stone. He paints "word pictures," as it were. He sculpts plots instead of statues. O. Henry, the short story writer, used to call his pieces "thumbnail sketches." This was a good term, because it was a compelling simile.

One feature common to much fiction is that it requires a "suspension of disbelief." Many plots are fantastic, in that real life people don't really get involved in the adventures described, but the reader ignores this because he's seeking fantasy to pass the time or gratify his emotions. People read fiction mainly for entertainment, and thus are prepared to accept otherwise unbelievable plots.

Many of the fiction pieces, especially the genre ones, satisfy the need for "conquering hero" fantasies. People read them to identify with the central figures, who are usually dominating, masculine types who win in the end despite severe hardships. This is most apparent in the "macho" hero types of stories, such as the "Executioner" series of novels, and the many private detective short stories and books. Western stories are classic hero fantasies.

There are genre books aimed at the female market, as well. The various stereotyped romance novels satisfy needs for love and tenderness. Like their male-oriented counterparts, they tend to follow strict formulas. The plots are similar, and only the names and places are different.

Genre fiction has gotten a bad reputation because some of it is trashy. This will almost inevitably lead you to the suspicion that you could do better. You probably could, but may not get a chance to try because the writers churning out the trash are already there. They made their contacts before you did.

Genre fiction does not have to be pulp magazine trash, however. Many genre pieces are written by people who are also talented novelists. The Swedish "Martin Beck" mystery series, written by Maj Sjovall and Per Wahloo, provides a good example of a novelist and poet teaming up to produce detective novels that are also serious literature.

The mechanics of plot construction is the subject of many theories. Any college course on creative writing features an instructor who can tell you all about it. The value of any particular theory of plot construction coincides with whether or not the person presenting the theory has been published or not. It stretches credibility to hear a theory expressed by someone who can tell you how to do it, but hasn't been successful in applying it himself. Few college instructors are successful novelists. Campbell Black (*Hangar 18)* is an exception. So was the late Glendon Swarthout, who wrote *They Came to Cordura.*

One feature common to most plots is keeping the reader in suspense. This is what keeps his interest throughout the piece. The writer must immediately build a mystery, laying out a situation while withholding certain facts to keep the reader wondering how it will all turn out. This is true of all fiction, not just the crime and mystery genre, but the mystery is the major part of the plot in a crime novel.

Selling fiction can be a serious problem. Many very talented authors were rejected at the start of their careers. Upton Sinclair found that his novel, *The Jungle*, was rejected five times before he placed it. Zane Grey also found that a famous, old-line publisher gave him thumbs down on his novel, *Riders of the Purple Sage*.

Are editors accurate judges of good fiction? Not necessarily, and certainly not always. One researcher produced typed copies of a novel that had already been a best seller to the tune of 400,000 copies. When he mailed it off to the major publishers as an unsolicited manuscript, he found that they all rejected it, including the publisher that had put it out in the first place.

The main point here is that often presentation is more important than the contents. A contribution by an unknown will get the attention of an assistant to the junior editor, or some other flunky. A novel or short story by an established author will get more respect, and more careful consideration by one of the true decision makers. As we see in other types of writing, editors like to deal with known quantities, and also tend to give less serious attention to newcomers.

Fiction is art. This is the overriding fact, and this is why the fate of a fictional piece is so unpredictable. One editor will reject it, perhaps condemning it as trash. Another will pick it up and go for it, and it turns out to be successful.

There truly are no rules. Fiction does not even have to be grammatical, or have a coherent sentence structure. Some published authors have written "experimental fiction," and had it published.

There are some trends, however, and it's wise to note them. Generally, successful fiction includes some careful research. When the story takes place in a real location, such as Los Angeles or rural Montana, it's necessary to describe the place accurately. The author who has been there and who can accurately record it on paper has the edge. On the other hand, the author who mistakenly locates Kennedy International Airport in downtown Manhattan will appear ignorant.

In other instances, it's necessary to describe accurately some technical facts, and the author without the specialized knowledge is handicapped. Some authors have made their reputations on meticulous research to support their fictional works. Ernest K. Gann, who was an airline pilot, drew upon his first-hand knowledge of commercial aviation and aerodynamics to produce *The High and the Mighty* and subsequent novels. Joe Poyer writes both fiction and nonfiction, and careful research is part of his work in either case.

Many novels are based, to some degree, upon the author's experiences. Describing places and events one has seen is easier than inventing them totally. It also lends authority and credibility if the author was engaged in the same work as his characters, within limits. We don't expect convicted murderers to write novels, and in fact almost none do, but there are several police officers who have written crime novels. Joseph Wambaugh is one, as we've seen. Dallas Barnes is another.

In many instances, though, the fiction writer can get by with careful confabulation. An author who writes about events in a foreign land may have never been there, but neither have most of his readers. A talent for making events on paper seem real is the crucial skill, and this will often make the difference between being accepted or rejected.

We find some truly outstanding instances of fiction with inaccurate detailing when we look at crime stories. Some mystery writers tell of revolvers with silencers. Some don't even know the difference between an automatic and a revolver.[1] Other authors state that revolvers have safeties.

Writers in the private detective genre often have the private eye investigating a crime that is properly the concern of the police, when in real life a private investigator who did this would find his license revoked. If he persisted, he'd wind up in jail for interference in police matters.

Some fictional cops will taste a powder found at a crime scene, and state "It's cyanide.", or "It's cocaine." No real-life police officer will ever taste an unknown substance. He'll package it and send it to the forensic laboratory for analysis. If he needs a quick answer, he may use one of the disposable test kits available on the police market. These can determine the presence of various illegal drugs, but are not substitutes for laboratory analyses.

We also see the fictional or TV cops kicking down doors when in real life they're much more cautious. There might be an armed and dangerous felon behind that door, waiting to "smoke" the first cop who comes through. The fictional shootings sometimes have the victim picked up and thrown across a room by the force of the bullet. In real life, simple physics dictates that the bullet does not have enough momentum to pick up and throw a victim across a hallway, much less a room.

Where does all of this leave you? Perhaps you have a talent for fiction and would like to try it on for size. If so, be prepared for some disappointments. The rejection rate is high, and you'll need lots of patience and persistence.

Two Plots

If you want to try your hand at writing fiction, here are two plot ideas for you. I thought them up but never tried producing a short story or novel with either because I don't have the talent it takes to write an inventive piece of fiction.

The Virus — The British Army's biological warfare department developed a new strain of flu during World War I. Winston Churchill, who was even then a very influential figure, pushed the secret development of germ warfare, to retaliate against the Germans, who had introduced poison gas in 1915. This primitive effort was crude but very contagious, and the British released it over the German lines in 1918, despite warnings by scientists that it might easily spread out of control. Several British pilots were recruited for this top-secret mission, and one night they sprayed the Germans with the virus. The disease spread rapidly, and infected both soldiers and civilians on both sides of the lines, resulting in the great flu epidemic of 1918, which killed millions of people. Horrified at the results and afraid that its role in the deadly fiasco might come out, the British Government imposed total secrecy on the project. The British Secret Service arranged for the scientists with knowledge of the project to die in contrived accidents to ensure their silence. The British Military arranged for the pilots who flew the mission to be assigned to dangerous missions where they were all killed.

If you decide to use this plot, you might begin by having the descendant of one of the scientists or pilots find a stack of old letters telling of the plot in his attic. From there, he gradually unravels the plot, despite efforts by the government to silence him.

The Man Who Had Nothing to Lose — A man very dissatisfied with the degeneration of society had resolved that, if ever he contracted a fatal illness, he'd undertake to eliminate some of the people who were responsible for the problems. At age 50, he learns that he has only six months to live, and as he has nothing to lose, embarks upon a campaign of killing various corrupt politicians, radicals, and crooked businessmen who, in his view, had done serious damage to the United States. He chooses a businessman who had narrowly escaped conviction for bribing a government purchasing agent, and stabs him in a parking lot, taking his wallet to make it appear to be a robbery. His next target is a corrupt government official who has just finished serving a too-short prison sentence for his crimes, and who lives alone. One night, he rings his bell and puts a bullet through his head when the former official answers the door. The police have no idea who is doing the killings, both because he works carefully and because he had never confided his plan to anyone else, thereby eliminating the danger that someone might inform on him. He succeeds in eliminating several dozen people before he either dies of his illness or is caught because of a mistake.

You can make this a contemporary story, unlike the previous historical plot. If you write it skillfully and keep the plot moving, you can make a gripping novel out of it, much like Frederick Forsyth did with *Day of the Jackal*.

Submitting Fiction

When submitting a fiction book for consideration, never send the entire manuscript at the outset. No editor will ever read it completely at this stage. It's best to send an outline of the story and the first few pages, to determine if you can generate any interest. If the editor asks to see the rest, send it to him, and keep your fingers crossed.

If you're trying short stories, you can send the entire story, as long as it's not over ten pages. This won't tax an editor's attention span.

Because fiction is pure art, you'll find that it carries with it a peculiar hazard. You'll probably face requests to revise it according to the editor's instructions. This is one of the problems that comes with the territory.

In this regard, it's vital for you to understand a particular distinction. If an editor tells you, that yes, he'll publish your work on condition that you revise it in the way he tells you, you stand a good chance of seeing it published. On the other hand, if an editor rejects it for a specific reason, don't be misled into thinking that if you revise your work to comply with his thinking you'll see it published. Ask first.

It's best to shop around with a fiction manuscript. Trying to revise it to suit every whim will run you ragged. In dealing with an editor who offers criticisms and suggestions for improvement, the one best way to handle the situation is to "qualify" him. Write or phone him, thanking him for his suggestions. Then ask him politely if he'd accept your piece if you make the changes he suggested. The odds are that he'll find an excuse, which immediately tells you something about the value of his suggestion. This is your cue to try elsewhere. It's very true in fiction that "one man's meat is another's poison."

Notes:

1. *The Fifth Angel,* David Wiltse, (New York, Pocket Books, 1985). On p. 222, we find the curious phrase, ".45 automatic service revolver." A few sentences be-

fore, the author states that a 20-gauge magnum shotgun would knock a charging bear backwards. In actuality, a 20-gauge is a light shotgun, and might have enough power to knock over a rabbit. Even a 12-gauge shotgun would not knock over a bear.

Chapter Twenty Two
Do You Need an Agent?

Literary agents have been with us for generations, and continue to thrive. We see advertisements for literary agents in writer's magazines, and some of these ads are legitimate. We also see articles in these magazines extolling the advantages of using agents. This is not surprising, as agents support these publications with their advertisements.

What's the real story behind using agents? The theory seems to be that an agent will help the author sell his material, and will negotiate higher fees and royalties, which more than offset his fees. Agents operate on a percentage, usually around 10 percent, and this is supposedly an incentive to do what they can to increase their clients' incomes. Agents allegedly also help their clients understand the verbose contracts written by publishers, and in so doing help their clients avoid the legal pitfalls set by devious publishers.

One hard fact is that agents get flooded with manuscripts from inept writers looking for miracles. This is why many legitimate agents no longer advertise. The responses to their ads are mostly literary "junk mail," unmarketable material by people who simply lack the talent.

Enter the fake agent. This is the killer shark whose stock in trade is "reading for a fee." Charging a newcomer a fee for reading his manuscript was originally a defensive measure by legitimate agents who could not afford the time to read everything that came their way. Reading bad manuscripts all day and sending them back to the authors doesn't normally bring in any income, unless the agent charges for reading time. This is why agents started charging previously unpublished authors fees.

When such a manuscript arrives at the office of a legitimate agent, it doesn't get the best treatment. The top staffers are busy dealing with the real moneymakers, and the newcomer's chaff is diverted to a junior member of the staff. In one sense, this is justifiable, because it doesn't take much savvy to recognize unmarketable trash. Often, the first few pages tell the story. However, the truly talented writer has no assurance that his manuscript will be read by anyone who can recognize his talent. In that regard, he's in the same position with a publisher, but the publisher doesn't charge him a fee.

The fake agent advertises that he'll read your manuscript for a fee (between $50 and $300), evaluate it, try to market it, and provide advice for its revision if necessary. Obviously, if he can collect one fee, he'll try for another, and this is what brings about the cruel deception. The fake agent doesn't tell a client that he's wasting his time. On the contrary, he'll "stroke" him, telling him that he has a brilliant, but unpolished, talent, and that he, the agent, can help him rework his manuscript to become a best seller. Each time the client sends him his manuscript and a check, he'll get it back with some notes scribbled in the margins and a letter telling him that the next revision should do it. This game will continue until the client runs out of money, credulity, or patience.

What, then, can an agent do for you? Actually nothing when you're a beginner and need his help the most. When you most need the contacts and when you most need professional advice is when an agent is least likely to help you. No agent will be interested in you unless you're already established, in which case your need for him and his services is far less.

Some of the big name authors work through agents, but only as a convenience, because they can't be bothered doing the legwork to market their manuscripts. They feel that their hours are better spent doing what they do best, writing. Their agent can do the tedious day-to-day work of querying publishers and hammering out the fine details of contracts. When you arrive in that league, you, too, might consider getting yourself an agent. Until then, do your own legwork, because this will provide valuable experience in dealing with publishers.

Chapter Twenty Three
Subsidy Publishers: Do You Need One?

Perhaps you have a book manuscript that you haven't been able to place. After trying many "trade" publishers, you may be considering a "subsidy" publisher. These are sometimes lumped together under the unkind term of "the vanity press."

Your need for a subsidy publisher will depend on two things:

- How badly you wish to see your name in print.
- How much money you can spare to shoot into the project.

What is a subsidy publisher? This is a publisher who'll publish your material on condition that you "front" the money to cover costs. This means that you take all of the risks, and if the publication doesn't sell, you'll lose your investment.

The bright side is that the subsidy publisher usually pays much higher royalties than does the trade publisher. He can afford to, as you've already paid his expenses and provided a profit.

What does your "front money" go for, anyway? First and foremost is his profit. He's in business to process manuscripts, and this must show a profit. He also has expenses, such as hiring readers to scan and comment on submissions. He has "account executives," a fancy term for salesmen, to liaise with the clients and sell them on the idea of having their manuscripts published by the subsidy publisher.

There are typesetting and proofreading costs, and he must also pay a layout artist to set the type into pages. Another artist designs the cover. There are also printing costs.

These involve process camera work to make the negatives. If there are photographs to accompany the manuscript, there will be halftone negatives to shoot. It then becomes necessary to prepare the negatives for platemaking, and this requires a specialist known as a "stripper." The stripper follows the page layout and makes up the "forms," the arrangements of negatives, known as "signatures" that serve to make the printing plates. If there are halftones, he lays them into their proper places. Finally, he "burns" the plates.

The pressman runs the job, turning out the required number of copies of the signatures. These go to the bindery for binding into book form.

This hurried description of what goes into a book will sketch in for you where your money goes. The physical preparations for printing your book take up the bulk of the costs. There are also some other expenses connected with promoting the book. The publisher may send free copies to book reviewers and the managers of bookstores. He may advertise it. How thorough a job he does will depend on how much money you have to sink into the project.

The difference between the ethical subsidy publisher and the shady one is the degree of encouragement provided. The ethical one will tell you flatly that he'll re-work your manuscript, set it up for publication, and oversee production if you pay the costs. The scam artist will insist that you have great talent awaiting recognition, and that your book's bound to be a success once properly presented to the critics and dealers. Some will even set up literary "parties" for you, at which the critics and dealers can meet you and even have you autograph a copy of the first edition! Don't be too thrilled at the thought of such a "party." It's a rip-off. You're the one paying the bill. You're also not likely to see many genuine literary critics or other truly influential people. They have no time for such foolishness, because they know that subsidy publishers rarely put out anything worthwhile. The ones who attend are likely to be marginal people and freeloaders who come to the party to tank up on the free booze and snacks. These people can't do you any good, even if they wanted to. However, some might ask you for your autograph.

There is one other important difference between trade and subsidy publishers, one that contributes greatly to the success of the latter. This is "T.L.C.," Tender, Loving Care. Trade publishers often seem inconsiderate toward writers. They're slow to answer, and when they do, their letters are sometimes laced with thinly concealed contempt. This is also true with magazines. By contrast, subsidy publishers send prompt personal replies instead of photocopied form letters, because their business depends on the goodwill of writers who pay them. This makes a powerful impression on a would-be author who is discouraged by the unenthusiastic reception he's gotten from others.

If you're serious about writing, you should be honest with yourself and in fact be your own severest critic. This is especially true if your manuscript has been rejected several times by trade publishers. Ask yourself, especially before considering a subsidy publisher, "Is this crap really worth publishing? Is it worth it for me to sink five or ten thousand dollars into it?" If your work has been rejected by a dozen or more trade publishers, you should start suspecting that perhaps they're right.

You may have an oddball manuscript hard to place with trade publishers, despite its intrinsic worth. If this is the case, you ought to consider self-publishing, which we'll cover in the next chapter.

Chapter Twenty Four
Self-Publishing: Is it Worth the Effort?

If you've decided not to go with a subsidy publisher, you should consider self-publishing. Some writers make self-publishing work for them, and the concept is worth a look.

Self-publishing is the alternative considered by writers who want to keep a greater share of the income generated by the sale of their books. If you decide to self-publish, you'll provide the front money to typeset and print your book, and you'll also have the responsibility of marketing it, shipping it to buyers, and collecting payment. Self-publishing can work for you if you're willing to do this, and willing to accept the risk of failure. If your book doesn't sell, for whatever reason, you'll lose your investment. You can also lose a part of your investment if you have too many copies printed.

The size of the press run presents a dilemma. Unit cost goes down with a longer press run, provided you sell all copies ordered. A typical press run is 1,000 copies, because it's very uneconomical to print fewer copies. However, if you can sell only 500, you lose half of the money you paid for the printing. Likewise if you're overly optimistic and order 10,000 copies, but sell only 3,000.

If it does sell, you'll find that administrative tasks cut sharply into your writing time. You'll have to place advertisements, take orders, ship the books, and collect the money. Some successful self-publishers have found it necessary to hire people to handle the volume of orders. In one sense, this is good because it means that the book is a successful moneymaker. On the other hand, hiring staff means that you become involved with personnel problems, including the risk of lawsuits by unhappy employees. One way to avoid this is to employ only family members. This allows you to side-step many personnel problems.

If you decide to self-publish, you'll need more skills than the ones required for writing a manuscript. You'll have to know the technicalities of layout and printing, including finding a bindery. You'll have to be familiar with type fonts, pagination, and selecting a cover style. You'll have to do your own cover artwork, or hire a commercial artist to do it for you.

You'll have to learn how to write a winning ad, to attract customers. This is an art in itself, yet some writers can do it proficiently.

The payoff is that you'll receive all of the income your book generates. If you can manage your production and selling expenses, you'll be able to realize a greater percentage of your book's sales as profit, compared to the royalties trade publishers pay.

The Internet has self-publishing services. These will print copies on demand, which means that you do not have to commit yourself to paying for a press run of a certain size. Two reliable web sources are:

www.iUniverse.com

www.Buybooksontheweb.com

Self-publishing is not for everyone. For the writer who has the knowledge and skills required, and who is willing to accept the restrictions, it can be profitable and satisfying.

Chapter Twenty Five
Reviews

If you do much writing, sooner or later you'll encounter a reviewer. In one sense, everybody's a reviewer, from the editor who decides whether or not to accept your proposal to the reader who buys the publication. You'll find people passing judgment on your work at every stage, but for this discussion let's stick to two sorts of reviewers: the person who writes a letter to the editor or to you about your work, and the professional reviewer who writes a review of your work for a publication.

The Letter Writer

All sorts of people read, but relatively few write letters. It also seems to be characteristic of American letter writers that they tend to criticize, not praise. The person who likes your work is far less likely to write to your editor about it than the person who doesn't. This "goes with the territory," and you should accept it philosophically.

It's also very rare for an author to write a critical letter about another's work.[1] There seems to be a tacit understanding that authors are simply out to earn a living, and that tolerance is the best course. Nobody's perfect, and in any event an author isn't paid to examine another's work for errors.

Publications don't pay for letters, even when published in a letters column.

Sometimes the letter will be so harsh as to fall into the category of "hate mail." There are a few people who write positively vitriolic letters, as if personally offended by a book or article. There are basically two ways to handle such letters. One is to ignore them. The other is to write a gracious note, thanking them for their views, but noncommittal in any other way. The worst course is to reply in kind. It may be very tempting to write an equally nasty letter back, but it's counterproductive. You get paid only for material published, not for letters to fans or critics. You must also consider the prospect of a letter of yours "making the rounds." When you receive a nasty letter, try to imagine it with your signature at the bottom. Would you like a note such as that to be passed around and seen by others? It would be very damaging to you. This is because your editor will look at it differently from the way you do. From his viewpoint, and the reader's, you're representing the publication, as well as yourself, when you write to a reader. If you write a nasty and ungracious letter, it reflects upon the publication.

The Reviewer

If your work is important enough to rate mention in a review column, you ought to be flattered and thankful. For an author, there's nothing worse than being ignored. This is why some authors slant their work to be controversial and sensational to gain attention.

Nobody loves a critic. At least, the ones whose work he criticizes don't love him. However, getting an unfavorable review is one of the risks of the trade. It's still better than nothing. Here's why:

The reviewer generally states his reasons for disliking the article or book he reviews. His readers may or may not agree with them. Remember that there are some reviewers who are so negative that they have developed reputations that anything they dislike must be good. Good or bad, the review publicizes your work.

What should your response be? If the review is favorable, a nice letter to the reviewer can only do you good. A simple thank-you note is one way to do it.

If it's unfavorable, don't do anything! Do not, repeat, NOT write a nasty letter in rebuttal. A negative review may sting, but resist the temptation to retaliate, even if the reviewer's totally wrong about something. If the reviewer made an obvious mistake in his review, such as an easily demonstrable error of fact, you may write a short and polite letter to his editor pointing this out. Otherwise, leave it alone.

A nasty reply to an unfavorable review is unprofessional, and will only harm you.[2] The reviewer will surely not be the only one who reads it. So will his editor. The reviewer may even show it to other editors and even to your colleagues. He also may refuse to review any of your future works.

Feedback from Critics and Letter-Writers

Critics can be valuable. Sometimes they're right. Reading their statements carefully can give you valuable guidance for your future writing. This leads us to another valuable point. If someone criticizes your work, and is correct, write a polite note thanking him or her for pointing out your error. State that you're only human, but that your errors go down in black and white. This sort of gracious treatment can turn an enemy into a friend. A simple and practical tactic is to include your home address and to state that you'll be happy to hear from him in the future. This may deflect a future critical letter from your editor to you. You're better off getting the letter yourself than having your editor receive it, and possibly publish it.

Notes:

1. An author did once write a letter to one of my editors. He disagreed very strongly with something I'd written. His letter was two pages, single-spaced, and was snarling and denunciatory in tone. The letter, in statements and language, was so extreme that it provided a laugh for the editor, myself, and the various other people who got a chance to read it. It was surprising to find such a well-known author writing such a missive.

2. I have worked both as an author and as a reviewer of others' works. Reviewing can be a thankless job, but it pays. In one instance, I received the second edition of a book to review. The author had, in his introduction, referred to someone (not myself) who had given his first edition an unfavorable review by calling him an "ass." The second edition was longer than the first, and worse. I had to give it a very unfavorable review. This brought a four-page letter in reply. The letter attacked the publication, attacked the editor, attacked my professional judgment, and attacked me personally. It was amazing that an author would go to this trouble to compose such a long and nasty reply, but I guess it takes all kinds....

Chapter Twenty Six
Some Important "Don'ts"

DON'T ever tell an editor that he ought to like your work because he's published worse. You may not get a reply to this because your letter will wind up in the circular file. This is the mark of the amateur, and can only offend.

DON'T ever write a letter to an editor to criticize another author's work. This implies a criticism of the editor's judgment, and editors don't take kindly to this. Another effect is that a criticism can make needless enemies. Many publications forward critical letters to the authors for comment or reply. That author may be an editor someday, and authors have long memories for this sort of thing.

Yet another reason is that your motives are automatically suspect. An editor will wonder if you're trying to build yourself up by tearing someone else down. This happens often enough for editors to consider it as a motive whenever they see any criticism of.one author by another.

One would-be author was crass enough to write exactly that. He sent a four-page, single-spaced letter to the editor of a magazine, tearing down an article and the author with it. The letter had a strongly denunciatory tone, and ended with a statement that the letter writer would very much like to write for that publication. As it turned out, he never got the chance, nor has he been published elsewhere.

Another author sent little notes to the editor, criticizing a contributor whom he saw as his competitor. The editor, who had a sense of fair play, knew that the critic and the other author were acquainted, and he did not take kindly to this back-stabbing. He not only revealed to the intended victim what his "friend" was doing behind his back, but he also saw to it that the back-stabber never wrote again for that publication.

DON'T ever write a nasty letter to a reviewer who writes something negative about your work. Be thankful for the attention. In writing, even negative attention is better than being ignored. Taking a reviewer to task (remember, he's only doing his job) will cause unpleasant ripples, and you can be sure that he'll remember your name, and perhaps pass it on to others.

DON'T ever have a confrontation with an editor unless you're sure that there's nothing more for you at that publication. You can't win a confrontation because even if you're right, you lose. There's only one thing worse than losing an argument with an editor: winning one. He may never forgive you.

If you truly feel that you have nothing to lose because you absolutely can't work with him, or if you're convinced that he's so unfair that it's not worth working with him, then you may take some pleasure in "telling him off."

It's a sign of emotional maturity, however, to defer satisfaction in the hope of having a chance of proper revenge down the road. You may someday be an editor or publisher, and be in a position to return the favor.

Better yet, it's preferable to avoid the confrontation by out-thinking the editor. There are many ways to do this, if you try. Pausing for reflection before confronting an editor will often show you a way out.

DON'T ever send out a query or manuscript more than three times without revising it. If three editors reject it in a row, there's something wrong with it, although the reasons that various editors give may not agree. If you can't see anything that might be causing a problem, let it lie for a few months, then try again. The work might be good, but the timing wrong.

Timing is often more important than authors may realize at first. Think of timing several months down the road. An Easter manuscript should be ready to go in January to meet many publishers' deadlines.

If you decide to revise it, try a change of title first. Look the text over carefully. Another title might be more truly descriptive, and help you sell your manuscript.

Success in a writing career is not only a combination of basic skill and good luck. It's also avoiding some basic blunders that can seriously impede a career. Most of these points are just "common sense," and are easy to understand.

Chapter Twenty Seven
Ethics

It may seem cynical, even useless, to discuss ethics in writing and publishing after a discussion that has dealt with many unethical actions. However, most writers, editors, and publishers observe a code of ethics, although they don't all agree on what it should be. Let's lay out a tentative code of ethics, supported by the majority in the field, as a rough guide.

There are several major prohibitions:

- *Don't plagiarize.* Copying another's work verbatim, without quotes or attribution, is plagiarism. This can get you sued if the work you've copied is still under copyright. Otherwise, it can get you a bad mark if your editor or the other author finds out.[1] It is often permissible to paraphrase, with or without a footnote for attribution. Much depends on whether you're using the work as an authority to support your own position, or whether you're adopting it as your own.

- *Don't try to sell the same manuscript to two different outlets at the same time.* This is definitely a no-no because it can get two publishers entangled in a copyright fight. It will rebound upon you if one or the other notices the same work in the other publication.

- *Don't attempt a major deception.* This includes a misrepresentation of your work. If you don't have an "exclusive," for example, don't claim that you do. A deception can be by commission or omission. It is as dishonest to fail to tell an editor a material fact about your work or the circumstances surrounding it, as it is to tell an outright lie. He'll feel abused and misused either way. It will do no good to claim that he simply drew an erroneous conclusion, as he'll resent having been fooled. Remember that editors have big egos. If you puncture an editor's ego you do so at your own peril.

■ *Don't "burn" your sources.* You may find some people telling you things in confidence. Indiscretion can hurt them, and also hurt your reputation. Keep in mind that this is so important that news media people have gone to jail rather than reveal their sources. "Burning" a source has an effect much more far-reaching than the immediate incident. It chills the relationship between many confidential sources and their writers. Many of your colleagues and competitors will be hurt if you "burn" a source, and they'll hate you for it. You may be unaware of this at the time, but you'll feel the effects many years afterwards.

There are also some minor points to watch:

■ *Be careful when you're dealing with a popular topic.* Try not to give the appearance of stealing ideas. This is sometimes impossible to avoid, but avoid it if you can. Seeming to steal another author's ideas can rebound on you a long way down the road. The aggrieved party may be an editor someday, and he may have a taste for revenge.

■ *Also be discreet when selling two manuscripts dealing with the same topic.* Some editors may interpret this as selling the same one twice, even though you've struggled to paraphrase the second one and even re-write it from a different slant.

- *Don't make promises that you can't keep.* Also try to keep the ones you do make. A good example is a commitment to meet a deadline. You can't "burn" an editor too often with this without causing great resentment. Failure to meet a deadline may be due to circumstances beyond your control, but forgiveness and understanding go only so far. You need to avoid creating an image of even minor dishonesty.

The Image of Honesty

It's equally important to also appear to be ethical. This means not getting involved in anything that can produce an image of unethical behavior. Trying to sell your work as an "exclusive," if you think it may not be, is chancy. Writing "facts" that you did not verify can explode in your face, if someone can contradict you decisively. As we've seen, failure to meet a deadline can also seem damning.

If a problem arises, it's best to contact an editor or publisher and disclose it before he confronts you. This produces an appearance of open-handedness and honesty.

The reason that image is so important is that, in publishing and writing, offenders are rarely sued or put on trial. A suspect has little or no opportunity to prove his innocence. He stands convicted, sometimes without his knowledge, and he suffers the consequences without knowing why.

Some think that ethics are a bore, and that "nothing succeeds like success." This viewpoint is pure expediency and opportunism, and it sometimes works. More often, it causes the opportunist problems.

Possibly the most important point regarding ethics is that it's simply good business. People generally expect you to be ethical, and will tend to distrust you if you're not or if you give the impression of being untrustworthy. This is very important when you have a good relationship with a publisher or editor who treats you well. These are few and far between, and jeopardizing such a relationship for temporary expedience is foolish.

Notes:

1. One author wrote a book that included a photograph I'd used in an article two years before. His caption was inaccurate in describing the photograph, and he did not give me credit. When I contacted him, he stated that he had asked the magazine's editor for help, and that the editor had sent him an envelope of previously published photographs. This author used the photographs indiscriminately, without thinking of the effect this might have on his reputation.

YOU WILL ALSO WANT TO READ: